Developmental Deviations
and Personality

DEVELOPMENTAL DEVIATIONS AND PERSONALITY
Theoretical Issues and Therapeutic Applications

By **Dov R. Aleksandrowicz**
and
Malca K. Aleksandrowicz

Gordon and Breach Science Publishers
New York London Paris Montreux Tokyo Melbourne

Gordon and Breach Science Publishers

Post Office Box 786
Cooper Station
New York, New York 10276
United States of America

Post Office Box 197
London WC2E 9PX
England

58, rue Lhomond
75005 Paris
France

Post Office Box 161
1820 Montreux 2
Switzerland

3-14-9, Okubo
Shinjuku-ku, Tokyo
Japan

Private Bag 8
Camberwell, Victoria 3124
Australia

Library of Congress Cataloging-in-Publication Data
Aleksandrowicz, Dov R.
  Developmental deviations and personality.
  1. Child psychopathology.   2. Child development.
  I. Aleksandrowicz, Malca K.   II. Title.
RJ499.A415   1989   618.92'89   88-21224
ISBN 2-88124-298-7 (Switzerland)

To our indefatigable teachers,
Orley Kathleen, Anna and Dan David,
who shared with us the mysteries of childhood

CONTENTS

Preface

The ideas presented in this book arose from dissatisfaction. Our work as a clinical psychologist and an analyst presented us with persistent problems that did not fit into our theoretical framework as they should have. One of these problems had to do with the influence of the parents on a child's personality and especially on psychopathology. Some parents we saw were so grossly disturbed or hostile that one justly expected the children to be ill. At the same time, other parents of very disturbed children did not fit either the children's pathology or the internalized parental image in the child's mind. Such discrepancies cast doubt on the trustworthiness of our reconstructive work with adult patients.

The other troublesome issue was a degree of uncertainty as to the therapeutic effects of insight. It is a well-known fact that seemingly well-timed interpretations do not always produce the expected effects. If a symptom fails to be resolved, will more of the same medicine accomplish the task? This issue of treatment impasses and difficulties has received considerable attention in psychoanalytic writings, but does the literature cover all the possibilities?

Our work in the field of infant development, employing the Brazelton Scale (1973), and later with infant-mother enrichment groups (Aleksandrowicz & Aleksandrowicz, 1987a), helped us understand the issues of innate individuality and of developmental aberrations. Working with infant-mother pairs is an exciting experience for an analyst, comparable to time-travel for an archeologist. It means observing and participating in the unfolding of a process, i.e., shaping of an object relationship and budding of personality, which requires years of labor to reconstruct in therapy. This experience with infants, as well as clinical work with children affected by learning disabilities and other developmental impairments, led us to join the ranks of clinicians who search for innate factors to complement psychodynamic formulations. This book is the product of our search.

Psychoanalytic investigators do not, as a rule, explore the role of innate developmental factors and only a few detailed cases have been published. Clinical studies of learning disorders take it for granted that restoration of learning skills should be the primary goal of treatment and amelioration of emotional problems is seen as a precondition for educational success. This implicit assumption is not always justified by clinical evidence. In some subjects affected by innate impairments the disorganization of emotional development and of object relationships is far more disabling than the learning deficit. In such patients, setting educational rehabilitation as the primary goal can cause more harm than help. Our book, therefore, aims to fill the gap between psychoanalytic and educational approaches.

We are indebted to our colleagues and students who shared their experience and ideas with us and to the public health nurses whose enthusiasm and skill were crucial for the success of our infant-mother enrichment groups. Most of all, we are indebted to the patients who helped our groping attempts to unravel the complexities of their emotional lives and gave permission to use the clinical material.

List of Cases

Psychoanalytic Psychotherapy of a Borderline Child with Deviational Development: Prologue*

When Uri's former therapist found a note saying that Uri had called from a military base, she became concerned. Was the phone call a signal of distress? Could this sensitive youngster make it in the rough world of the military service? Her concern was understandable, because most of Uri's early childhood had been an unrelieved misery and his treatment stormy and arduous. As it turned out there had been no reason for concern after all: Uri learned that the therapist had recently moved to a city near his base and called to tell her proudly that he had been admitted to the IDF Air Force Academy, the most selective and demanding flight school of all.

Looking back at Uri's therapy we believe that its success and the stability of the treatment gains were due to an integration of psychoanalytic and developmental insights. The analytic approach was applied to interpretation of conflicts and defences. The insight into developmental pathology helped to understand the aberrations of emotional development and their impact on Uri's self-image and family interaction. The diagnosis of deviational development was crucial in building up and sustaining a therapeutic alliance with the child and his parents, and relieving a sense of perplexity, impotence and hopelessness which dominated the family atmosphere. Understanding the deviational development and its impact was also

* Reprinted, in a revised form, from the International Journal of Psychoanalytic Psychotherapy, 1975, 4:410-423, by kind permission of Jason Aronson, Inc.

essential to mobilize the considerable resources with which the child and his parents had been endowed.

Therefore we present the case of Uri and his treatment in detail to illustrate the practical as well as scientific need to integrate psychoanalytic and developmental approaches.

A. Reason for referral

Uri was referred for treatment because of enuresis at the age of nine. There were other problems too: morbid envy of his thirteen-year-old sister, temper tantrums at the slightest frustration and perseveration. If he stuck to a topic, for example, Jeeps, it was "Jeeps" for breakfast, lunch and dinner until the whole family dreamt at night about "Jeeps"....

His scholastic achievements and social adaptation at school were good. He was particularly interested in math but refused to paint, sing and write stories.

B. History and family background

Uri started his life as a second born and after his mother had a miscarriage. While pregnant with him, mother again had some bleeding and was confined to bed for a few weeks but Uri was born at full term. According to mother, Uri was a "strange" baby. He slept most of the time, but when awake he was not very responsive nor was he cuddly. At one year of age he was a chubby boy and began to walk, but stopped and began again at eighteen months.

His peculiarities were clearly noticed at the age of eight months when the family visited an out-of-town relative and Uri spent the entire day in the strange place screaming; he stopped only when the family reached home. From then on he developed a deep fear of strangers which persisted for years to come. Other peculiarities became apparent too: Uri did not allow anyone (including his parents) to pick him up or hug him and maintained distance from people. When strolling his head was bent down, eyes cast on the pavement. He demanded that "sameness" be maintained, and reacted with fear and anger to changes in his immediate environment. Uri was terrified of moving objects such as ceiling fans or the scales in the super-markets and was very sensitive to noises.

At the age of nine months he developed a fear of being left alone in his crib and for ten consecutive nights refused to go to sleep until heavily sedated. Subsequently, until the age of five, he woke up almost every night, at times screaming.

Training for cleanliness began at eighteen months. Uri re-sisted; mother fought but gave up. He would retain his feces for two to three days and then excrete in his pants. This pattern continued well into his fifth year. He stopped wetting during the day around his fourth year, but remained a bed wetter.

Uri began to talk at the age of two-and-a-half to three, and the parents could not recall any peculiarities in his speech. He showed a remarkable memory for numbers and dates. He was also very musical and, at the age of four-and-a-half, began to play the piano. He quit after six months, but would become very agitated when his sister missed a note or if anyone in the household sang off key.

At the age of three, Uri began to attend nursery school. He would not play with the other children nor sing or paint; instead, he spent most of the time with different mechanical tools. When interrupted, Uri would throw a temper tantrum. At that time, he also began to collect keys of different sizes and functions. His conversation was almost exclusively around this topic and every acquaintance brought him keys. All in all, he had two hundred keys.

At age five, he was hospitalized in a psychiatic ward for one week because of his "key mania" and other peculiarities and was diagnosed as having "Minimal Brain Dysfunction." His EEG showed a partial suppression of the regular rhythm, parti-cularly on the left side, with irregular activity of 4–6/sec., more pronounced posteriorly and on the left side.

At five, Uri started to attend kindergarten. His interest in keys declined and Uri now occupied himself with numbers and dates, irritating everybody with this topic. However, he began to sleep better and also became more sociable.

A new problem appeared: accidents, first a cut requiring emergency treatment, then frequent bone fractures and cuts.

When Uri was asked to do something contrary to his wishes (or when the sameness was disrupted), he would react with screaming or with a physical attack. This led to violent clashes with the mother particularly in regard to body contact. Mother bathed, soaped, combed and even kissed Uri, despite his resistance, well into his tenth year.

The constant struggle between Uri and his family finally brought him into therapy.

C. Parents

Father, a gifted, intelligent man, was the administrative director of a large general hospital. He was described by mother, by himself (and later when observed by the therapist) as a kind, loyal, warm person, but very anxious and passive (though not in his work). In his role as a father, he appeared weak and preferred to withdraw rather than confront the problematic son.

Mother was an attractive, intelligent but unsophisticated housewife with only a high school education. She was the kind of woman "who knows that she wants," has her own views about the upbringing of children, and is not easily swayed by new educational fashions. However, she was not rigid and could accept reasoning. Mother was also quite aggressive in a sarcastic way and embittered about being forced into the controlling role in the family. She preferred her daughter who was described by the parents as "normal" (in contrast to Uri), a compliant, sweet, uncomplicated girl.

D. Adventures in psychotherapy

Uri was a beautiful boy with a slightly oversized head, blond curly hair, and big round brown eyes with an expression of curiosity and naiveté, reminiscent of St. Exupery's (1943) "Little Prince".

He came to the first therapeutic session reluctantly but immediately opened up almost shouting at the therapist: "I am a bed-wetter and I am sick and tired of it. Every morning I must rinse my sheets, but that is not what bugs me. I am angry because on weekend mornings mom, dad and my sister sit down to the breakfast table while still in their pajamas; I am the only one who must change because they say I stink."

In the first few sessions Uri expressed his envy and anger at the sister and told about a recurrent traumatic dream (its relation to the sister became apparent only later on): "A black water boiler is hanging over my head and about to explode." Uri also talked about his fear of the buzzing sound of the fluorescent lights and of thieves. He did not allow his father to leave the therapy room and, in the presence of the latter, without any inhibitions, inquired about "facts of life." The topic was pursued in the next few sessons and Uri expressed his deep fear of thieves, robbers and empty spaces. One day he declared, "I have not wet my bed in the last three nights," and clearly waited for a compliment. Instead, the therapist commented that she likes Uri whether he is wet or dry because Uri is a likeable boy. Taken by surprise, Uri admitted, "I am not always so likeable," and continued to describe his mischievious behavior, letting his imagination loose and plunging into aggressive sadistic fantasies.

At the next appointment, he was angry at the therapist: "How come," he complained, "I have been here already six times and last night I again wet my bed?" Quickly calculating Uri's age, the therapist responded: "Well, you are 78,840 hours old. Do you expect to be cured in six hours?" Uri accepted the mathematical reasoning but demanded that the therapist predict the exact time needed for the cure. To this request he was told that the therapist was not a god who can perform miracles. After the role of the therapist was redefined, Uri was reminded that the success of the therapy depended on his efforts, too.

Thus we touched upon the problem of the therapist's lack of omnipotence, which soon led us to discuss Uri's thoughts of grandeur. In the next few sessions Uri dedicated most of the time to glorifying his wristwatch (anti-magnetic, waterproof, Swiss made), while at the same time belittling the therapist's watch. Resistance mounted, but Uri continued to come reluctantly, and kept on talking about the same topics: idealizing one object or person (e.g., a neighbor's dog, the teacher) and belittling another (the therapist's dog, mother). He was confronted with the explanation that in order to "feel big" he has to make others look small. The motive of "My watch is better than yours," was interpreted on the level of castration-fear, i.e., Uri's body is more complete and thus better than the female's body (sister, mother, therapist). An outburst of anger was Uri's reaction to this interpretation, but the next association had to do with sister's vagina "which is red like a bleeding wound." The therapist by then had realized that an angry response to an interpretation indicated the acceptance of the interpretation which, in turn, produced further associations or even an actual change in behavior.

After two months of therapy a new topic appeared— suspicion. Uri inquired constantly whether mother discussed his secrets or shared mutual secrets with the therapist. He was still bed-wetting and the time was now ripe to give him a new interpretation: wetting was his body's way of telling him that something was so terribly frightening that Uri refused to even think about it. Instead, his body speaks for him. To this Uri volunteered the explanation that something bad may happen to his penis and that by urinating in bed he "checks" the state of his penis. And then Uri spoke about his mother's "meanness" and her threats that "If you keep pulling the penis you are bound to have wounds." It was then suggested that bed-wetting was also a way of punishing mother while at the same time masturbating. Uri's loud voice attempting to drown the therapist's voice, assured the latter that the interpretation was correct.

During the next few sessions Uri dealt mostly with his feeling toward his parents: If mother was positively described, father was negative, and vice versa. The main complaint against father was his weakness and overanxiousness. The complaint against mother was that she prefers girls and loves sister more than Uri. The "splitting" to "all good" or "all bad" was particularly clear in the family therapy session (which took place approximately once a month) and the origins of "splitting" as a defence mechanism were pointed out.

Around this time there was an increase in Uri's compulsive masturbation at any time and circumstance, and mother warned and threatened. Uri was convinced that masturbation would result in the loss of his penis. The therapist rejected this hypothesis, supplying Uri with the interpretation of castration fear as it is perceived by little boys—and little girls—and, of course, the purpose of the female sex organs for reproduction. Uri rejected this explanation but brought up the topic of his intense envy of his sister and expressed his wish to be a quiet, self-controlled child. When offered the interpretation, "You want to be like your sister so mother will love you as much or more," Uri became angry and started bossing the therapist around, reasserting his omnipotence.

The topic of omnipotent thinking became again the center of therapy in the next few sessions, while resistance to deal with it was at its peak. Uri's need to control the environment was so strong that he even became infuriated when the cabinet door handles in the family's kitchen were changed from red to black, and complained that they were black before so why keep changing. The therapist explained to Uri that his need for sameness was a remnant of his past and asked him why he wanted things to remain unchanged, to which Uri answered: "I guess I get frightened when things are no longer the same. I guess 'cause I lose control over them!" He was then asked if being an almighty king was really such a good bargain. Uri admitted that it was not—kings are above everybody; therefore they don't have any close friends. They are lonely and envied but not really loved, and Uri wanted so much to be loved. But Uri was still far from accepting the fact that he was just another mortal.

At home, clashes with mother were a daily routine. Old problems were now revived. Uri accused mother of trying to poison him with her "broiled liver," and demanded only soups or desserts. Besides the problem of constipation, bed-wetting recurred.

The family was gathered for an emergency family therapy session and the session, as usual, started with mutual accusations. The therapist pointed out that it was neither Uri's fault that he was born so sensitive and consequently was difficult to handle, nor was it the parents', who did not know how to cope with Uri and tried every possible approach. After this statement (which was repeated in practically every family therapy session) tension was reduced and the family started to work constructively.

Uri was confronted with the interpretation that he refuses to grow up—he wants to stay a baby who eats liquids, lies in his urine and retains his treasured feces. The mechanism of projection was also explained to him. But the anxiety kept on mounting and he suspected a man in the bus station of approaching him. (It was, however, not entirely clear whether the man was in fact a pervert who responded to Uri's inquisitive eyes or whether the whole incident was just a paranoid delusion.)

During the time of Uri's intense projective preoccupation he also became extremely sensitive to dirt (or supposed dirt) and to almost indiscernible odors, dramatically expressing his disgust by spitting on the floor as if he was ridding himself of a noxious substance. Interpretation concerning reaction formation to dirt as well as the origins of his projection were loudly rejected; in light of Uri's known sensitivities from his infancy, he might have actually experienced those odors more intensely than other people.

One day Uri inquired whether circumcision could cause leukaemia. Not realizing the full implication of his question (since Uri was always worried about disease), the therapist just reassured the anxious child that leukaemia is a rare disease entirely unrelated to circumcision. That day, while running after a ball, Uri was hit by a car. His leg was fractured in two places and Uri had to stay in the hospital for one month. The therapist visited him there and found a frightened little boy with a thigh-high cast on his leg.

When Uri returned to therapy, he recounted several incidents of being almost overrun by cars, "and you see," he bragged, "I was not killed." Again the interpretation of his thoughts of omnipotence was offered; again he became aggressive, but now he was asked why he reacted with anger when his immortality was challenged. Uri did not respond but the following session he brought a dream: "Mother is on the staircase, a thief comes and snatches her purse; she offers him money, he takes the money but snatches the purse too and runs away." Uri brought a number of associations leading to a conflict around his sex organ; that is, a conflict around acceptance or rejection of masculinity. The "snatching hand" in the dream is the same hand that was once fractured. "It is now stronger and quicker than before," and with this hand Uri can play tennis "better than Dad."

At first, it sounded like a typical Oedipal fantasy; however, the "thief" in the dream stole the purse for his own body as well, and the meaning of it was revealed by association to the next dream. Uri saw "a black dog snatch something from my hand." Again, at first glance, the dream expressed castration fears; however, it led to a more complex bisexual fantasy. Uri asked what happens to a fighter pilot who needs to urinate while flying at the speed of Mach one. Does the pilot urinate in his pants? Since the therapist was silent, he himself answered: "The pilot must urinate in his pants or else he will die because his penis would become stiff and dry up. The dirty water in the kidneys will go up into the stomach, fill it up and then the stomach will explode, unless, of course, the bad water can come out through the penis." And so Uri described his fear regarding erection and why he would immediately attempt to undo any by urinating.

Therapist and patient now spent hours analyzing thoughts and fears in regard to the bisexual identity conflict. Consequently, Uri was beginning the process of accepting and redefining his sexual identity. He was now less afraid of physical closeness to people of either sex. One day he stood very close to the therapist while his hand was busy scribbling. It suddenly dawned on the therapist that Uri wanted her to touch him. And so, for the first time since psychotherapy began, the therapist put her arm around Uri's shoulders. He did not move; he wanted to be hugged! A few days later, the father came with tears in his eyes and told the therapist that Uri had asked to be loved and even kissed father for the first time in Uri's life.

At that time, the full-length cast was removed from Uri's leg and replaced by a walking cast. Uri was worried lest his leg become short or crooked. He was also depressed, did not eat well, could not concentrate on his homework, and had difficulty falling asleep as well as waking up. During this convalescence, Uri became completely dependent on his mother for all his bodily needs. He also refused to stay alone at home. One day he sadly commented, "It is good to die. A dead person does not have to worry about pain anymore. Grandma is seventy years old. She is lucky, she does not have much time to suffer, she will soon die." Uri spoke about the advantage of leaving this world, concluding with a heartbreaking matter-of-fact statement: "I am so different from the other children, I am really nuts and always will be." The therapist asked him if his friends thought so too. No, they did not, Uri responded; as a matter of fact, they visited him often and even begged Uri to play with them. The therapist pointed out that even though Uri was, in some ways different from other children, it did not necessarily make him "bad", "crazy" or less lovable.

And then Uri brought another dream: "A thief was standing near my sister's bed. The therapist illuminated him with a flashlight and the thief disappeared, became a *bone*, and only a shoe was left of him—a new blue shoe like my sister's shoe." The association dealt with his incestous feelings, his guilt, and the punishment of becoming a skeleton. However, the "thief" motive repeated itself here too. Uri wanted to steal his sister's shoe-vagina. Uri also wanted to be a girl. He repeated the accusation that his mother preferred girls since she liked his sister better.

Resistance now reached a new peak. Father had to force Uri to come. First, Uri ran out of the room, after a short while returned and started accusing the therapist of plotting against him, then he physically attacked her. The therapist had to twist Uri's arm backward so that every movement on Uri's part hurt him. She then interpreted his aggressive act as appropriate for an infant and that the attack was actually directed against his mother who he perceived as "bad" whenever he perceived father as "good." Thus Uri was confronted with his "splitting" defense mechanism. Gradually he relaxed and the therapist let go of her grip.

The next session Uri was almost apologetic and he said: "I am sorry, I did not mean to hurt you. I just wanted to show Daddy that I am not afraid of you—that I am on his side...." Uri now expressed the wish to marry his father. That night he could not urinate and he screamed in terror "that it was burning there"; consequently a physician was called in. He gave the boy some Valium which Uri suspected might poison him. His behavior was increasingly dominated by projection and again the roots of his projection were interpreted to him.

He then spoke about the contradictory wish: On one hand, he wanted to be a boy, proud and happy with his penis; but being a boy also meant being aggressive and nasty and unloved by mother who preferred the quiet, obedient sister. So in order to be loved by mother he had to give up his masculinity. But giving up his penis and becoming pregnant meant death because the "dirty water" would fill up the stomach and it would explode. The dream about the "exploding water boiler" now became meaningful. Giving up his masculinity had another advantage; it could prevent the dangerous competition between father and son.

Uri was reexperiencing acute Oedipal conflict, but two obstacles were hindering its successful solution: (a) Uri had not outgrown his narcissistic wish for omnipotence which he projected and experienced as a terrifying threat from an almighty father; (b) father was not a perfect model for identification.

In the next few weeks Uri struggled with the problem of identification, trying gradually to pull together all of his father's qualities, assets and shortcomings alike, into one unit. Uri was trying to see his father as one whole object.

At that time, Uri was overcoming many fears. He went to the dentist and had his cavities filled without even a local anesthesia, while in the past general anesthesia was needed. He took swimming lessons (before, he refused to go into deep water) and was about to participate in a swimming competition. Four hours before the competition, however, Uri ran, fell down and fractured his hand.

He came with the new cast, smiled apologetically, and explained that this was the same hand he had once fractured on the hospital grounds. It turned out that his first accident occurred at the hospital where his little cousin, a four-year-old boy, was dying of leukaemia. Uri was forced by mother to visit this cousin. The cousin died, explained Uri, "because he was a bad boy and God took him away." Uri then expressed his fantasy that if he hurt himself, God would not be angry with him anymore and would not take him away as he did the cousin. The issue of the Oedipal conflict was taken up again. Uri's fear lest father do unto Uri what Uri wants to do unto father was tied in with Uri's infantile thoughts of omnipotence. The next few sessions dealt with Uri's struggle to find an adequate solution for his Oedipal conflict. From time to time, Uri fell back on primitive defense mechanisms and particularly on projection. Other areas of functioning were successfully mastered: He was now a top student in school and was now willing to express himself in singing, painting and writing stories; Uri was also liked by both teachers and students. The relation with his sister also improved. He was no longer so morbidly envious of her. He became closer to father and they shared some activities. The clashes with mother diminished. Uri also began to play a musical instrument; he joined a children's orchestra and within three months caught up with the most advanced students.

The last half year of therapy was dedicated to the consolidation of acquired insights and the new, more adequate patterns of behavior. Uri understood that his exceptional inborn sensitivity was no fault of his and realized that his parents' behavior was often a reaction to his own. Uri now accepted both parents as people made of opposing qualities. "Splitting" was no longer a necessary defense mechanism.

At this time, in family therapy, the therapist insisted that mother stop bathing the boy and increase her physical distance from him, thus in a sense freeing him from her excessive maternal indulgence and overprotection. Encouraged by the therapist, she found a part-time job. At first, Uri resented the fact that he had to come home to an empty house and at times had to prepare a sandwich for himself. However, within a few weeks he became used to his independence and even took pride in his increasing responsibilities.

Close to termination (about two years from the beginning of therapy) the therapist suggested that Uri undergo psychological tests and an EEG. Uri turned out to be "a bright child with a high intellectual potential, anxious, with somewhat weak controls and a trace of organicity. . . ." The EEG was normal. A few days after the test, Uri, who had never left home before, joined his Boy Scout troop for a one-week campout. When he returned, he came to say goodbye to his therapist. She then asked him if he had been worried about bed-wetting. Uri looked at her, smiled, and teasingly said: "What kind of a psychologist are you anyhow? Don't you know that I quit wetting a year ago!"

E. Discussion and conclusions

On reviewing Uri's history one is struck by the gradual but dramatic change around the age of five. The withdrawn, peculiar, panic-stricken child who lived in a world of his own began to develop social relationships, and participate in age-appropriate activities, albeit at the price of phobias, temper tantrums and family conflicts.

Mother seems to have played a major role in Uri's adjustment to reality. Mother was not a "patient", accepting person. As a matter of fact, she was a strong-minded, controlling and aggressive, yet warm woman, who did not give in to Uri's way of life. Never allowing Uri to withdraw, she insisted on physical closeness, nor did she give in to Uri's food fads. The family regarded Uri as somewhat peculiar, but they followed the mother's example and expected from Uri what they would have expected from a normal child.

Father gave in more to Uri's demands and terrorizing, to avoid head-on collisions. Mother was disappointed at father's weakness and angry at him for shifting Uri's education onto her. Consequently, there were bitter clashes between the two on this specific topic (which also became the focus for other marital disagreements). Had we not known about Uri's early development, we might have been tempted to construct a pathogenetic hypothesis for Uri's problems as follows: An agressive, controlling, ambivalent mother; a weak, withdrawing, anxious father; marital problems; and Uri, being a sensitive child, would be seen as the victim of this pathological environment. A closer analysis, however, revealed that Uri's sensitivity, detachment and odd behavior dated from early infancy and might well represent symptoms of brain dysfunction, which was documented later. Therefore, we may assume that *Uri's inborn characteristics* elicited conflict-ridden parental attitudes and set in motion a vicious circle of a disturbed relationship. In his latest book (1973), Kanner says: "Making parents feel the guilt of responsibility for their child's autism is not only erroneous but cruelly adds insult to injury," and this statement may well be applied to families of all children with deviant development.

It is quite plausible that the energetic behavior of Uri's mother, far from damaging the child, actually helped to pull Uri out of his autistic world, though at the price of building up a borderline personality whose functioning depended extensively on "primitive" defense mechanisms (Kernberg 1968, 1975). The role played by primitive defense mechanisms had a considerable influence on the course and handling of therapy. Initially, the therapist reacted to the manifest Oedipal material (which consisted of both the "positive" and "negative" relationship), but, as we went along, the pre-Oedipal conflicts came into the foreground and more primitive defenses were revealed under the guise of Oedipal wishes.

The most conspicuous regressive defense was represented by Uri's thoughts of omnipotence manifested also by disregard of danger. When Uri's recklessness and accident-proneness were analyzed, it became apparent that they served a dual purpose. One was to relieve guilt and to head off fears of death or castration (e.g., his question, "Does circumcision cause leukaemia?"); the other purpose was to reassure Uri of his immortality ("You see, I was not killed").

Idealization and devaluation of the love object were other prominent mechanisms also related to the grandiose-narcissistic state. Uri's attitude toward the therapist was one of boundless admiration, bitter envy and defiant depreciation: "My watch is better than your watch." Uri's self-concept vacillated between pathetic feelings of worthlessness ("I am nuts....") and bragging. The idealization-devaluation also led to *splitting* into the "all good" and "all bad" object, which culminated in a physical attack on the therapist in order to gain father's affection.

Uri's omnipotent, grandiose fantasies and wishes have to be understood as compensatory attempts to cope with severe narcissistic injuries incurred as a result of grossly deviant development. This not only resulted in a distorted, negative self-image, but also hurt the relationships with his parents. His feelings of having been loved less than his sister were based on reality; it is not easy to remain affectionate, when the child rejects physical contact, screams or becomes immersed in incomprehensible activities.

The last line of defense was represented by *denial* and *projection*. The denial was often apparent when Uri's grandiose aspirations were challenged. Projection led to transitory delusion: fear of being approached by a homosexual, accusations of poisoning against the mother and complaints of evil smells. The delusions may have been facilitated by Uri's unusual sensitivity to such stimuli as noise, movement and smell.

As these primitive defenses emerged, the therapist found herself forced to modify the treatment technique. Uri's intense attachment was manifested by an overwhelming negative transference, and accuracy of interpretations was more often than not confirmed by Uri's uncontrollable rage. The therapist felt that holding back interpretations because of the partient's intense resistance and loss of reality judgment would lead nowhere. Moreover, it could have cast her in the role of the father who capitulated in the face of Uri's rage. She therefore went on persistently interpreting the negative transference, challenged the reality distortions (mainly within the treatment situation itself) and pointed out how Uri's rage was provoked by any threat to his narcissism and how he used it to terrorize and manipulate the environment. The direct challenge of primitive defenses meant that she had to absorb intense aggression and at times had to control Uri physically. She was reassured, however, when she saw the patient becoming more relaxed and warm following such violent confrontations.

One more comment about Uri's aggression: It was provoked not only by a narcissistic injury, but also by any attempt at physical closeness. Therefore, it seems probable that Uri, with his insecure ego boundaries, perceived closeness as a threat to his individuality; the fear of fusion mobilized aggression which allowed Uri to keep a "safe" distance, albeit a lonely one.

It is therefore possible that the decrease of aggression was brought about by the gradual clarification of his sexual identity and acceptance of his masculinity which, in turn, helped to strengthen his self-identity and ego boundaries. The more primitive mechanisms could be discarded, thus allowing for a better ego integration.

Summing up, it seems that Uri's emergence from his autistic world was encouraged by his mother's firm attitudes and consistent behavior. From there on, Uri moved into borderline personality organization with "the pathological condensation of pregenital and genital aims under the overriding influence of aggressive needs" (Kernberg, 1968). The parents could not cope adequately with this situation. Mother expressed her ambivalence openly, father in a more subtle way by withdrawing. Uri reacted to their behavior, and the whole family was trapped in the vicious circle.

Psychotherapy was aimed at arresting the merry-go-round, thus letting off its participants. The success of the treatment was facilitated by Uri's desperate wish to be "like the others" and by admirable family cooperation.

And so "The Little Prince" finally descended from his lonely star to join the crowded world of ordinary people.

CHAPTER TWO

Developmental Deviations and Psychopathology

A. What is a "developmental deviation?"

We use the broad term "deviation" intentionally because we refer to a wide variety of idiosyncratic developmental patterns that may influence the formation of personality. The case of Uri illustrates the need to take such idiosyncratic developmental patterns into consideration when dealing with patients whose development had been irregular or impaired.

B. Innate temperamental qualities

The first group of developmental deviations consists of unusually pronounced manifestations of "normal" temperamental traits.

The studies of Escalona (1968) and of Korner (1964) on innate individual differences and those of Thomas et al. (1968) on temperament in infants brought into focus the individual variability in infants and its significance. Freud (1937a) wrote about the importance of innate individual characteristics and stated that "we cannot specify their nature and what determines them." This is no longer so. We know much more about the complexity of infant behavior (Wolff, 1966; Osofsky, 1987) and have tools for measuring the individual differences (Bayley, 1969; Brazelton, 1973; Aleksandrowicz and Aleksandrowicz, 1967). The innate temperamental differences influence the way in which an infant experiences his world and influence the behavior of the caregivers (Thomas et al., 1968; Korner and Grobstein, 1967; Aleksandrowicz and Aleksandrowicz, 1975, a and b). Few people will smile to an infant who is unresponsive, or resort to soothing maneuvers which consistently fail to produce any effect. Temperamental traits refer to *how* people act and think, e.g., slowly or quickly, rather than *what*. Traits like activity, tempo and vigor, are relatively stable features (Escalona and Heider, 1959; Kohlberg, 1969; Ausubel and Sullivan, 1970). Other innate characteristics such as irritability or "cuddlinesss" (Brazelton, 1973) seem to be less stable over the years, but have, nevertheless, significant influence on the emotional development and early object relationships (Korner, 1964, 1971; Schaeffer and Emerson, 1964).

Temperamental idiosyncrasies cannot be classified as clinical syndromes and therefore are not represented in DSM III (1987) or any other standard diagnostic classification. Their impact on personality formation and maladaptive functioning in later life, however, is considerable.

C. Lags and impairments

The second group of deviations consists of developmental lags and circumscribed impairment of perceptual, motor or cognitive functions. In theory one ought to differentiate between developmental lags, i.e., delayed appearance of a function, and minor neuropsychological deficits. In clinical practice, however, the separation is often unclear. Functions that are delayed frequently remain relatively weak, either because the child avoids practicing an activity that is fraught with frustrations or because the delay is a forerunner of a neuropsychological deficit. For this reason it is convenient, as far as our discussion is concerned, to group developmental lags and circumscribed deficits together.

Developmental lags and neuropsychological deficits are listed in DSM III on Axis II, with the exception of Attention Deficit Disorder which is an Axis I syndrome. The DSM III classification reflects current concern with learning disabilities and consequently academic skills figure prominently on the list. In clinical practice, however, we find that circumscribed neuropsychological impairment may well lead to serious emotional consequences, even though the academic performance is satisfactory. This is particularly true in the case of very bright children who may perform below their true potential but still well above the level of their less endowed peers. In these children the presenting symptom is usually emotional or behavioral, and only a painstaking examination reveals the neuropsychological difficulty.

The DSM III classification refers to *global, complex* functions, such as reading or language. It does not attempt to ferret-out the underlying *specific* deficit, such as impairment of sequential auditory memory, right-left discrimination, spatial orientation or inter-modal integration. Emotional development, however, is often linked to such specific neuropsychological functions more than to global areas of functioning.

In summary, we take a much broader view of developmental deviations than that reflected in standard nomenclature. The common denominator of such developmental deviations is that they appear early in life, are intrinsic, that is, innate or due to very early environmental influences, and are presumably biological in nature.

D. Clinical studies of developmental deviations

The clinical literature dealing with temperamental differences is scarce; even Lichtenberg (1983) in his exhaustive review of infant research and psychoanalysis does not discuss developmental individuality. Fries and Woolf (1953) presented cases illustrating the effects of "congenital activity type" on the development of personality and formation of symptoms, and Aleksandrowicz (1975a) described the treatment in a case of temperamental "mismatch" between mother and child. This patient, a vibrant, restless child, has now become a gifted dancer and choreographer, a vocation that expresses well her true nature (Aleksandrowicz et al., unpublished).

The clinical literature dealing with emotional effects of developmental lags and impairments is not much richer than that dealing with temperamental endowment. Developmental pathology is common: most surveys of hyperkinesis report prevalence of 6% to 15% or more (Wender, 1971) and learning disabilities are estimated at 6% (Gillberg et al., 1982). Rubin et al. (1972) claim that 40% of children with behavior problems in school show signs of subtle neuropsychological impairments. In spite of such staggering figures, very few investigations deal with the emotional sequelae of developmental pathology (Weil, 1978, 1981; Aleksandrowicz and Aleksandrowicz, 1975b; Palombo, 1979, 1982). P. Kernberg (1982) and Palombo (1982) linked some cases of borderline syndrome in children to "minimal brain dysfunction", and Murray (1949) and Andrulonis et al. (1982) suggested the same hypothesis in regard to some adult borderline patients. Lack of awareness as to the role of developmental impairments is not confined to psychoanalytic and psychodynamic literature. Lishman's (1987) exhaustive textbook of organic psychiatry does not even refer to learning disabilities or attention deficit. Hyperactivity is mentioned but once in connection with epilepsy.

There are some illuminating clinical reports of psychotherapy of patients with circumscribed neuropsychological deficits, but they are rare. Small (1973) described the history and therapy of such a patient, and Palombo (1979) treated a learning-disabled adolescent. Pine (1985, pp. 189–191) described clinical vignettes illustrating the emotional impact of learning disabilities, and Aleksandrowicz (1975b) published the treatment of a borderline child, which we described in Chapter One.

This book reviews systematically the influence of developmental deviations on personality and the clinical significance of that influence. In the chapters that follow we examine the direct and indirect effects of developmental deviations and discuss the implications for therapy in general and psychoanalysis in particular. In Chapters Eleven and Twelve we discuss the implications of developmental studies for psychoanalytic theory; the last chapter is a summary of our findings.

CHAPTER THREE

Direct Manifestations of Developmental Deviations

Developmental deviations do not appear as isloated entities. To the contrary, they become incorporated into the structure of personality and exert a wide range of effects, some of them direct, some of them indirect and remote from the area affected by the deviation. For clarity's sake we will divide the manifestations of developmental deviations into five categories, even though in clinical practice these categories overlap to a certain extent:

(a) Direct expression of the deviation;
(b) Emotional reaction to the deviation;
(c) A defence mechanism or coping device to control or compensate for the developmental deviation;
(d) The effect of a deviation on a specific developmental stage;
(e) The effect of developmental deviations on parent-child relationship.

In this chapter we will examine some direct manifestations of devleopmental deviations. We will not review the whole range of innate perceptual and cognitive impairments which are the subject matter of neuropsychology. We will focus only on some common impairments that result in maladaptive behavior patterns and may easily be mistaken for conflict-determined, neurotic symptoms.

The differential diagnosis between innate impairments and neurotic symptoms is not always easy or clear-cut, because an innate temperamental trait or impairment may become interwoven into intrapsychic conflicts and inter-personal relations. Nevertheless, it is useful to recognize the innate core of a maladaptive behavior and to separate it from the dynamic superstructure.

The first category of maladapative ego functioning that needs to be examined is reaction to stimuli and impulse-control. A careful examination of inappropriate reactions and failure of impulse-control is one of the mainstays of the psychiatric examination and of psychoanalytic treatment. We speak of "acting-out" unconscious conflicts, of unconscious motivation magnifying the response and of displacement of affect from another, repressed context. The classic example is Wolf Man's inexplicably intense grief at the poet's grave, which was interpreted by Freud as displacement of the patient's repressed mourning for his dead sister (Freud, 1918, p. 23). The interpretation revealed the positive, affectionate aspect of Wolf Man's ambivalent relationship with his sister and became one of the cornerstones of Freud's analytic reconstruction.

Another common example of distorted response is transference. The therapeutic regression reactivates infantile yearnings and consequently minor events in the therapeutic relationship acquire symbolic significance and evoke an exaggerated or irrational response. It is these irrational emotions, fantasies and actions that alert the analyst to the emergence of transference and provide a lead to unconscious processes.

This basic premise, i.e., that an unreasonable, inappropriate response is always an indication of unconscious conflicts, does not apply to patients whose ability to control drives is impaired because of innate factors. Hyperkinetic children in particular manifest impulsive behavior, irritablility, affective lability and impaired inhibition of drives, i.e., behavior traits that may easily be confused with symptoms of emotional deprivation or acting-out of internal conflicts.

These personality traits of hyperkinetic children oftern persist after the patients have become adolescents and adults. Mendelson et al. (1971) reported that among adolescents who had been diagnosed as hyperactive children, 67% were described as irritable, 56% manifested temper tantrums and 39% complained of "low moods". Such patients are prone to overreact to emotional stimuli, but the tendency to overreact is more pervasive; less dependent on specific stimuli and situations, in contrast to dynamically-determined overreactions. Such patients also tend to overreact in several affective modalities, i.e., anger, sadness or elation all may be excessive.

When a patient reports that he or she had symptoms of hyperkinetic disorder in childhood, or manifests other signs of neuropsychological impairment, one ought to exercise caution in ascribing an unconscious conflict to any disproportionate or impulsive reaction. This may or may not be the case and only a careful scrutiny of each patient's personality and of each situation will provide a reliable answer.

Impaired inhibition of drives may be manifested in two ways. One is impulsiveness, i.e., a propensity to respond to stimuli without reflection. The other, related but not identical form of dysinhibition, is an inability to delay or forego the gratification of an instinctual need when the provocation, or temptation, as the case may be, becomes intense. The drive may be aggression, genital sexuality or greed. The response may be impulsive, but it may also be deliberately delayed and well-planned. The characteristic feature of this behavior is the subjugation of all the psychic forces, such as ego-ideals, values, and the subject's other affectionate relationships to one overpowering instinctual need. In particular, such subjects seem unable to consider the full implications of their actions. When confronted with the nature of their action or faced with its consequences, they usually respond with intense anger, which then turns into depression, shame and a loss of self-esteem.

Romantic literature is replete with examples of reckless abandon to desire, revenge or greed, and such instances are not rare in clinical practice either.

Mrs. Q., a middle-aged married woman, a mother of three, and a respected business executive, was in treatment because of dysphoric moods, dissatisfaction with herself and obesity. She knew everything there is to know about diet and weight control, yet, when gripped by a sudden desire for food she would swallow bread, chocolate or cakes, to the point where she felt nauseated and disgusted with herself. Any discussion of the need to control her food intake or any comment about her weight would enrage her. She knew, however, how to contain and disguise her feelings most of the time, and she felt ashamed of them. The patient also reported uncontrollable shopping sprees of which she was ashamed, too.

During one of the sessions the patient said: "You know, I am ashamed to tell you that, but I suddenly realized that when anybody suggests a diet, I feel as if someone was taking the milk bottle away from me; I feel desperate and furious."

The problem of drive control in this patient was not limited to oral needs; this brief example, however, illustrates the issue.

It is not easy to decide whether such imbalance between drives and inhibitions is due to constitutionally excessive drives or to impaired controls. Both possibilities seem plausible. Although there is no method for measuring the intensity of drives, observation of infants demonstrates convincingly that some of them are endowed with vigorous needs and desires while others are more placid. In other subjects the hypothesis of impaired controls seems to apply because innate as well as acquired neuropsychological impairments commonly result in drive dysinhibition (Elliot, 1982).

It is important to emphasize that the clinical manifestations we describe here are *not* sociopathic personality disorders or cases of emotional deprivation. We are referring to individuals with a well integrated superego. This is not a failure of values or object relationships, but of ego's ability to contain drives.

Various perceptual or cognitive disabilities may find direct expression in a patient's behavior in an analytic session and be mistaken for resistance or neurotic inhibition. For instance, many children with attention deficit disorder manifest a rigidity of habits which may be taken for negativism. A learning-disabled child will often pretend that he refuses to perform a task out of rebelliousness in order to avoid the humiliating admission that he is unable to cope with it. "I would rather be bad than stupid," the child seems to be saying. An analytically trained therapist may accept the patient's defensive stance at face value, especially if the child is unquestionably angry and defiant, and overlook the underlying disability.

The problem of differential diagnosis between conflict-determined and innate impairment of function is illustrated by the following vignette:

> Mr. Y. was referred to analytically-oriented psychotherapy during a stormy and painful process of divorce. It soon became apparent that Mr. Y.'s disastrous masochistic marriage was a part of his self-defeating life-style and a continuation of a life-long submissive, masochistic attachment to his mother. A similar pattern of masochistic, passive-aggressive relationship began to emerge in transference.
> The effects of interpreting the neurotic character traits were very slow. The therapist became aware of a characteristic discontinuity in the treat-

ment process, as if progress achieved in one meeting would be partly
lost by the time of the following session. The patient complained that his
memory was poor, and attributed his forgetting of previous sessions to
it. Mr. Y.'s Bender Gestalt test showed superior visual memory, namely,
an exact recall of all nine figures, and the therapist, therefore, saw Mr.
Y.'s forgetting as part of his passive-aggressive resistance.

Mr. Y. himself provided the clue to his "repression". While in college
he developed a habit of jotting down every important lecture. He would
then study by memorizing *visually* the content of his notes. He could
recall each page, while his memory of the *spoken* content was hopelessly
inadequate. In other words, Mr. Y. suffered from impaired *sequential
auditory* memory, while his visual memory was excellent. Impairment of
sequential auditory memory is, in fact, a fairly common cause of learning disability.

Another innate characteristic which may raise issues of differential diagnosis is slowness. There is a wide variability in
the spontaneous tempo and rhythm of activity in infants (Kestenberg et al., 1971) and adults. Therefore, slowness may well
be an innate characteristic. Some subjects, however, report that
they act slowly in specific situations only. On closer examination it often transpires that those subjects suffer from minor
impairments, e.g. of attention or fine motor coordination, and
slowing-down serves as a device to reduce errors. In such
cases, therefore, slowness is an *adaptive* device. Such an adaptive slowness is a normal behavior trait in the aged, but may be
seen in young subjects with innate impairments as well. It is
very common in children with learning disabilities and may
aggravate their school difficulties considerably.

Finally, slowness may serve emotional needs, namely negativism, passive hostility and the wish to control. Some children, as well as some adults, have developed an exquisite
capacity for annoying everybody by simply doing anything
that is demanded of them, but doing it slowly. Slowness is also
an effective way to control: one need only to observe a whole
family packed and ready to go on a picnic, waiting, while
Junior is tying his shoestrings with maddening meticulousness.

Slowness, then, can be an innate characteristic, an adaptive
device, or a drive-motivated anal character trait. In a given
subject slowness may be an expression of any one, two or all
three of these determinants. In analysis it is usually possible to
tease-out the innate, adaptive and drive motivated compo-

nents. The latter, for instance, wanes and waxes according to the interpersonal situation, e.g., when the patient has a reason to be annoyed. The adaptive component becomes more pronounced under stress or threat, e.g., during an examination. An innate characteristic is relatively stable, though it may also increase during anxiety. Innate characteristics not only co-exist with acquired behavior patterns but also shape them. Korner (1971) pointed out that innate characteristics influence the *choice* of defences; therefore, a characteristic may well be an innate and a defensive trait in the same subject.

The last direct manifestation of neuropsychological impairment which we need to discuss is *rigidity*. Lack of flexibility is one of the cardinal signs of brain injury (Luria, 1973); in subjects with subtle neuropsychological impairment it is much less conspicous, but nevertheless can be observed in many subjects. Perseveration may be observed in psychological tests, especially the Rorschach, Bender and WAIS tests. The behavioral traits are inability to shift and "thinking in loops". The inability to shift was described by one patient who could not follow the changing topics of a social conversation. Another patient could not sustain a friendly contact with a child and conduct a serious, adult conversation at the same time. Some children are in the habit of making comments about a topic after the teacher has already started a new one. Another, very bright patient, described her desperate helplessness when dealing with relatively simple mathematical problems which involve inverse proportions, e.g., a pipe which fills a reservoir in *fewer* hours will fill up a *larger* part of it in one hour.

"Thinking in loops" is a term coined by a patient to describe her inability to detach herself from a train of emotionally charged thoughts, in spite of her better judgment and her wish to be done with the subject. Instead of feeling relieved after expressing her anger or anxiety, she would return to the topic again and again, each time with a greater intensity of affect, like a self-amplifying electronic circuit, until the built-up tension became unbearable. This kind of perseveration might be mistaken for an obsessive symptom. The difference lies in the intense, self-augmenting affect, absence of doubt, which is so typical of obsessions, and no indication of ambivalence. There is also no unconscious content to explain the symptom; it is simply an inability to deal flexibly with an emotionally charged situation. It is quite probable, therefore, that in those cases where psychoanalysis fails to resolve obsessive thinking, the reason is that the symptom is due to a neuropsychological deficit.

In conclusion, subtle neuropsychological deficits of cognition, impulse control and other integrative ego functions often bear superficial similarity to neurotic symptoms or signs of resistance. Attempts to resolve such disabilities by interpretation are futile and discouraging for the patient and the therapist alike (Small, 1973), and undermine the therapeutic alliance.

CHAPTER FOUR

Emotional Effects of Developmental Deviations

A child whose motor, perceptual or cognitive development is impaired or delayed is invariably a frustrated, angry child; he is usually also insecure, and lacks in self-esteem. In order to understand how this occurs we have to trace the relationship between emotional development and that of perceptual, motor and cognitive functions.

Emotional development revolves around the polarities of gratification and frustration. It is the loving, empathic care of the mother that assures the prompt satisfaction of physical needs, such as hunger, and of emotional needs, such as the wish for attention. Satisfaction of needs instills in the infant a sense of security, "basic trust" (Erikson, 1950).

Satisfaction of needs, however, is not always possible nor prompt, and the infant experiences frustration. If the frustration is not too distressful nor too prolonged it stimulates growth. The child learns to *anticipate* satisfaction and delay his need. For example, a hungry infant who was crying dejectedly a moment ago, will laugh at the sight of the familiar cup even before gulping the cereal. Anticipation occurs when the infant recognizes the signs of approaching satisfaction, hence anticipation involves a degree of cognitive organization. In this manner, the cycle of satisfaction and frustration stimulates cognitive growth. At the same time, however, anticipatory pleasure and the ability to delay gratification require a certain maturity of the perceptual and cognitive systems. In other words emotional development and perceptual-cognitive organization depend on each other.

Frustration also stimulates the child to find the means to overcome obstacles and satisfy his wishes; in this way frustration also stimulates cognitive and motor development. This happens, however, provided the child's efforts lead frequently to a successful outcome. If the child's efforts remain futile too often, the result is temper tantrums, or loss of interest, withdrawal and listlessness. Only the sequence of wish-frustration-effort-satisfaction-pleasure has a growth-promoting effect. Parental approval of the child's efforts and accomplishments, i.e., "mirroring" (Winnicott, 1967; Kohut, 1971) has a powerful reinforcing effect, but it should be emphasized that *successful performance in itself* is a source of intense gratification and a powerful reinforcer. Stechler (1982) described vividly the triumph of a toddler who finally accomplished a task on which she had set her mind. She then performed a "victory song" all for herself, ignoring her mother and the observer. Papoušek and Papoušek (1983) traced the pleasure of mastering a task to early infancy and related it to effective cognitive processes, such as recognition of a familiar percept, and intentional movements that produce an *expected* effect. The pleasure of mastering a task motivates the infant to repeat it and practice that specific function. In this manner he develops motor and cognitive skills and consolidates his sense of mastery over his body and over the environment. The sense of mastery, or competence, becomes an essential component of normal narcissism in the following way:

(a) An *effective* operation of an ego function is accompanied by pleasure;
(b) The pleasurable affect serves as reinforcer and leads to a repeated operation of that function;
(c) Ego functions that are repeatedly associated with a pleasurable affect become gradually invested with libido, and
(d) The libidinally-invested motor, perceptual and cognitive functions consolidate into a libidinally invested nucleus of self-representation, corresponding to Freud's "body ego" (Freud, 1923).

The young child soon learns that some tasks can be mastered and some cannot. That is the basis of reality-oriented cognition. He also learns that there is considerable lawfullness and predictability as far as the mastery of his body and the environment are concerned. This *predictability* of gratification and frustration contributes to a sense of stability and security. Parental behavior is also predictable within certain limits, i.e., the child expects that his basic needs will be satisfied and that some behaviors are approved and some disapproved. All this contributes to a sense of security.

In conclusion, a child's self-representation is a condensation of parental reflections ("mirroring") and of the child's self-experience, i.e., his effective and ineffectual functioning. If the affect associated with these two sources of self-representation was predominantly positive, the result will be a healthy, balanced narcissism and positive self-esteem. If self-experience, parental mirroring or both were predominantly negative, self-esteem will be impaired. An inconsistent, unpredictable self-experience or parental mirroring result in a confused, unintegrated self-representation and narcissistic vulnerability.

We will now turn to the vicissitudes of self-representation in the child with deviant development. The life experience of a child with developmental lags or impairments is characterized by a relative predominance of frustration over mastery, i.e., negative over positive affect. The frustration becomes more painful when the scatter between functions is wide. For instance, a bright child with poor motor development observes and understands his surroundings well and develops a wide range of mental images of tasks which he cannot perform effectively. We have observed that such toddlers tend to become over-dependent, insecure, expecting parental help or retreating at the slightest difficulty and over-reacting to frustration and disapproval.

The life of a developmentally deviant child is not only fraught with frustrations, it is also less predictable as far as success or failure are concerned. As the child grows older and the demands more complex he becomes increasingly bewildered by doing some tasks well and failing others. This uneven performance may be reflected in a seemingly inexplicable scatter of school grades (often mistakenly attributed to emotional factors), and is also well demonstrated in intelligence test profiles. One such subject told us:

"I could never tell beforehand what kind of reaction I will get from my teacher. Sometimes the teacher would praise my answer, saying, "that's a smart boy", or something of the kind. Sometimes he would look at me with amazement while all the other kids laughed. Obviously I must have said something very silly but I couldn't tell what. At times I wished I were dumb; that would have been easier."

The following example illustrates the emotional impact of subtle developmental deficits.

Mrs. C., a capable research scientist, experienced frequent moods of paralyzing anxiety and helplessness. During analysis it became apparent that her neurotic inhibitions were reinforced by minor cognitive difficulties of which she had been only dimly aware. She could deal effectively with complex and abstract problems, provided they could be put into a framework or that she could find at least a mental "foothold" from which to begin analyzing the problem. An unstructured array of data and correlations could throw her into a panic. This was related to her inability to attend to more than one stimulus; though a gifted amateur musician, she could not, for instance, play a piece in one voice and sing it in another simultaneously. The patient was deeply troubled by her erratic functioning and it engendered a sense of incompetence and self-contempt, reinforcing the masochistic traits of her personality. Insight into her difficulties led to a considerable decrease in anxiety and improvement in the patient's self-confidence and effectiveness at work. Eventually it also facilitated the analysis of the dynamic structure of her neurotic personality traits (see Ch. X).

We have studied self-esteem in learning-disabled children (Aleksandrowicz et al. 1988) and found it significantly impaired. Moreover, self-esteem was significantly *lower* in children with *higher* I.Q., a finding consistent with our hypothesis that self-perception, which is presumably sharper in bright children, is a basic component of self-esteem. Coopersmith (1967) also found a correlation between low self-esteem and a history of delayed walking, but did not elaborate that finding further. Weiss and her co-workers (1978) in their follow-up studies of hyperkinetic children into young adulthood found that the subjects' vocational adjustment and rating by employers were *not* lower than those of controls, but the subjects rated *themselves* negatively on such items as conventional ideals of social interaction and competence. Hence, the low self-esteem of those subjects apparently was not related to environmental factors, but to negative self-perception, a finding consistent with our hypothesis.

Many hyperkinetic children perceive painfully the inadequacy of their impulse control, affect modulation, and other integrative ego functions. Some older children or adults describe their childhood experiences in words like: "I was a freak", "I felt there was something wrong with my head", or "My thinking brain wanted one thing but my doing brain did something else." This perception of malfunction at the very core of the ego dates back to very early life stages and constitutes a deep narcissistic hurt.

In conclusion, the low self-esteem of the child with developmental deviations can be traced to a disruption of sense of competence, which causes a profound damage to self-representation and to the growth of normal narcissism. Moreover, developmental deviations are apt to have a negative effect on parental mirroring (Chapter Seven) and that causes further damage to the child's self-representation.

The second major emotional problem of the child with developmental deviation is coping with aggression. The child's attempts at mastery are persistently thwarted and the result is a pervasive and chronic anger. The anger may be diffuse, directed at the "whole world", it may be aimed at the parents and later at the spouse or other transference objects; it may also be directed against the subject himself. Such anger, however, does not remain isolated, attached specifically to the impaired function. It becomes incorporated into other areas of emotional development and object relationship. In some patients, this intense anger may be masked by a passive-dependent and controlling relationship; in others, it may find expression in a self-derogatory, sneering personality trait. Other patients express their excessive anger by a contemptuous devaluation of everybody else or by a petulant, querulent personality. The problem of aggression is further compounded in those patients in whom a neuropsychological disability involves an impairment of impulse control, e.g., in most hyperkinetic children (see Chapter Three). Such subjects tend to be impulsive, i.e., to respond rapidly, without reflection, their emotional responses tend to be excessively intense, and sometimes they seem unable to stop themselves once they give vent to their anger.

Mr. G. was a young adult patient whose detailed diagnostic evaluation, prior to analysis, revealed a previously unrecognized mild cerebral palsy. During analysis he described his violent childhood rages. Once, at the age of about eight, he became provoked by another boy who accidentally stepped over G.'s sand castle.

Mr. G. began to hit the other child with a belt; the buckle cut the other boy's face and he ran away bleeding profusely. Mr. G.'s father, usually a severe and overcritical parent, was left speechless and did not even attempt to punish the son. For Mr. G. himself, the incident remained a painful and frightening memory, a part of his self-image of "a small Hitler", as his father had once called him.

The excessive anger of the child with deviant development and the difficulty in coping with it in an adaptive way, persist into adulthood. The most direct expression of such senseless rage is found in the "Dyscontrol Syndrome" (Elliot, 1982). The problem may, however, lead to a massive compensatory reaction and manifest itself in a rigid, overly controlled personality (Weil, 1978), with excessive isolation of affect, or in an emotionally impoverished, "wooden", over-intellectual personality. Exploration of such character traits usually reveals defence against uncontrollable rage and a developmental deficit may be discovered as one of the factors leading to it. Some patients may not have excessive difficulty in restraining their behavior, but nevertheless experience overly intense affective responses to emotionally charged situations, a response which we call "affective flooding". The emotion may be negative (e.g., sadness, anger) or positive (e.g., joy, gratitude); its content may be quite appropriate to the situation, but its intensity is overwhelming. Such "affective flooding" brings to mind the global, undifferentiated motor and affective responses of the very young child and also the emotional lability of the brain-injured patient, but at this stage too little is known to venture a hypothesis. We know from clinical experience, however, that such "affective flooding" may lead to a variety of defensive and compensatory devices that become traits of the patient's personality.

Another significant emotional effect of developmental deviation is a propensity to anxiety. Weil (1978, 1981) described "panic-rages" in toddlers with perceptual hypersensitivity. These are presumably direct expressions of ego failure. In our experience excessive anxiety frequently stems from a dim, or sometimes quite conscious, awareness of the subject's unreliable impulse control and affect modulation. Such patients often

harbor fantasies of insanity and fear of loss of control. The
fear of loss of control experienced by patients with neuropsychological deficiencies is excessive but not entirely irrational.
It is a result of repeated frightening experiences of being over-
whelmed by ego-alien affects or impulses. The following case
illustrates the point:

> Mrs. J., was in treatment because of severe and disabling phobias.
> Analysis revealed ego deficiencies, especially in the area of impulse and
> affect control. In one of her sessions the patient described a visit to
> comfort a friend who had been experiencing a very unhappy life situa-
> tion. As Mrs. J. was listening to the account of her friend's misery, she
> was overcome by a feeling of sadness so intense that she had to excuse
> herself and leave precipitously. This was one of many such incidents.
> Mrs. J. enjoyed her work, but when it reached a certain intensity she
> would go into what she called "a high", a state of excitement, irritability
> and talkativeness, over which she had little control, and which made her
> fear for her sanity. Thus both painful and pleasurable affects tended to
> flood her and produce anxiety.

The anxiety caused by weakness of ego's controlling
mechanisms may co-exist with phobic anxiety. Indeed, in
many patients the two types of anxiety act synergistically, as
was the case with Mrs. J. (see Chapter Eight). There is a basic
difference, however, between a phobia and an ego deficiency.
Phobic anxiety is a defence against a repressed, forbidden
impulse and the anxiety-inducing stimulus represents the content of that impulse symbolically. Ego-deficiency anxiety is less
related to the specific *content* of the impulse than to its *intensity*.
The impulse though ego alien is not necessarily unconscious,
and the anxiety-inducing stimulus need not have any specific,
symbolic meaning. A wide range of emotionally-charged situations, which stimulate erotic or aggressive impulses induce
anxiety in such patients. In terms of psychoanalytic theory
phobic anxiety is primarily due to *dynamic* factors, while ego-
deficiency related to *economic* forces.

The difference manifests itself also in analysis. In purely
phobic patients an interpretation touching on the ego-alien
wish generates intense anxiety and mobilizes resistance and
defence mechanisms. Working-through of the impulse is experienced as a relief. In patients with ego-deficiency interpretation of content may evoke little resistance and have little

therapeutic effect, while a discussion of the patient's inability to control drives and his fear of madness is initially intensely threatening but becomes very supportive when it is worked through.

Another common emotional symptom in patients with a history of developmental deviation is a tendency to depression. In our experience depression in this group of patients is multidetermined. The most prominent factor seems to be a profound sense of estrangement from the primary love objects, going back into pre-Oedipal stages of development. One patient described her experience in these words: "My mother always told me that she loved me; I suppose she did, but she never respected or even understood my feelings. For that matter, neither did I understand hers." Korner (1964) suggested that some infants lack the ability to make themselves understood and Aleksandrowicz (1975a) described the treatment of a temperamental "mismatch" between mother and daughter, which culminated in a suicidal attempt by the little girl.

A sense of lack of competence is also a factor in the tendency to depression. The intense rage experienced by the frustrated impaired child becomes, in most cases, partially internalized and directed against the self, thus also contributing to depression, self-criticism, masochistic character traits or self-destructive behavior. Last but not least, there is also a possibility that a deficiency in the integrative central neural mechanisms in itself contributes to depression (Weil, 1981) even though at this stage of our knowledge there is no empirical evidence to support such a hypothesis.

In conclusion: a person with a developmental deviation perceives himself, however dimly, to be different, less competent in mastering his environment, less dependable in coping with drives, affects and inner conflicts and less emotionally consonant with his parents. Such negative perception of one's ego functions and the resulting narcissistic injury lead to a low self-esteem, negative self-representation, non-adaptive aggression, depressive tendency and a propensity to anxiety.

CHAPTER FIVE

Coping with Developmental Deviations

Children with an idiosyncratic endowment or a functional deficit learn to live with it and devise coping methods. Such coping methods can be divided into three broad categories: (a) devices to minimize the functional impairment, (b) defenses against impulse dyscontrol, anxiety and other emotional difficulties resulting from the developmental deviation, and (c) methods to cope with the narcissistic injury and negative self-representation.

A. Functional impairment

The most natural reaction of a child to recurrent frustration is to avoid the task which he or she is not competent to perform. We often hear about a child who "does not like to draw" or the youngster who "just is not interested in athletics and prefers to browse in the library". Such statements should not be taken at face value. We have yet to meet a small child who does not like to draw *if* he can, or an agile youngster who does not delight in physical activity. A declared "lack of interest" is a disguise for avoidance.

Once a subject has overcome the tendency to avoidance, he finds means, sometimes very ingenuous ones, to overcome or bypass the impairment. We have mentioned the student who memorized visually his notes, because he could not remember the lecture. Another subject, a bright high school student, suffered from partial anomia, i.e., could not recall words, although he recognized them, and had great difficulties in constructing sentences. This youngster taught himself to memorize whole sentences from textbooks and used them as "building blocks" to express his own ideas. Some exceptionally intelligent people, endowed with imagination and determination, turn their disabilities into assets. Unable to use conventional strategies to cope with a cognitive task, such as a mathematical problem, and unable to rely on guidance by teachers, they learn to depend on their own ingenuity and become capable of unconventional, creative ways of thinking. History of science is replete with problems which could only be solved when someone was able to disregard the basic premises of the conventional thinking of his time. Some of those original thinkers might well have acquired independence from conventional concepts while learning to circumvent their own cognitive limitations.

Cognitive detours and coping devices have clinical significance because they may be misinterpreted as neurotic behavior traits. For instance, some subjects, prone to become confused or disoriented because of impaired attention span or poor retention memory, compensate by becoming pedantic, "conservative", over-concerned with order and sameness, and anxious when forced to deal with change. Such character traits may easily be misdiagnosed as compulsive symptoms. They are not apt to change, however, unless the underlying cognitive impairment is recognized and the anxiety caused by episodic disorientation is reduced.

B. Defence mechanisms

Failure to control drives adequately and the ensuing anxiety mobilize defence mechanisms in individuals with developmental deviations as much as in other subjects. In Chapters Three and Four we have described the particular vulnerability of patients with developmental deviations to failure of impulse control. Some of them overreact and develop a "vigilant control of themselves and their surroundings" (Weil, 1978). Others employ common defence mechanisms, e.g., denial, displacement or reaction-formation, and manifest neurotic symptoms or character traits which result from these defence mechanisms. The neurotic symptom or character trait in such cases, however, cannot be attributed to a developmental deviation *alone*. In these patients analysis of the symptom invariably reveals at least two co-determinants: (a) a dynamic one, i.e., a repressed wish originating from early object relations and (b) a structural one, i.e., non-specific anxiety due to ego-weakness (Chapters Three and Four). The following example illustrates such symptom formation:

> Mrs. J. (whose analysis has been mentioned in Chapter Four) was suffering from phobias, particularly from an intense fear of situations in which she felt an irresistible impulse to commit suicide. This phobia expressed identification with her depressed mother, who had often threatened suicide and once, when the patient was 12 years old, made a serious suicide attempt. The symptom expressed also guilt caused by the patient's deeply repressed death wishes against her egocentric, unempathetic mother. In the patient's unconscious, any striving to become independent became immediately identified with the wish for her mother's death.
>
> At the same time the symptom was related to Mrs. J.'s neuropsychological dysfunction. She was painfully aware of and bewildered by her cognitive difficulties, i.e., momentary confusion due to attention deficit or occasional failure to deal with an intellectual problem which required "shifting" from one conceptual set to another. She was also threatened by her impulsive behavior and inability to contain affects. Her self-perception as an erratic, unpredictable "freak" made her unable to deal with the intrapsychic conflict, except by paralyzing anxiety or avoidance. Only when the cognitive and integrative ego difficulties were explored and the patient's self-representation consolidated in a more positive way, was she able to confront and deal with the issue of her deeply repressed hatred toward the mother.

The neurotic mechanisms adopted by patients with innate ego-weakness are apt to become excessively rigid resulting in "difficult" patients or "unanalyzable" personalities. In other patients the defence mechanisms are frail and prone to failure when the subject is faced with stress. In such cases we are faced with an episodic dyscontrol syndrome (Elliott, 1982) or borderline personality organization (Murray, 1979; Palombo, 1982; Andrulonis et at., 1982). In each case, however, understanding of the innate features of personality and exploring the neuropsychological dysfunction are essential for the treatment to be effective.

C. Narcissistic vulnerability

The devices employed for protecting narcissism are not, strictly speaking, defence mechanisms. The task of the latter is to assure drive control and reduce anxiety. The coping and compensatory devices that protect narcissism shield the subject from negative self-representation and depression. They range from highly adaptive and creative to grossly maladaptive and disabling personality traits.

Some gifted and determined individuals invest so much effort into the struggle with an impaired function that they become exceptionally proficient in that area. Demostenes was not the only one who turned a weak function, in his case a speech defect, into outstanding ability. We know subjects with delayed speech development and a history of verbal expressive difficulties in childhood, who have become unusually meticulous and adept in expressing their thoughts, and eventually developed an impressively lucid and rich writing style. In other words, an area of narcissistic vulnerability is turned into a source of narcissistic gratification.

Other coping devices are less adaptive. Some narcissistically vulnerable children seek comfort in the company of much younger children whom they can dominate, or in solitary fantasies of power and grandeur. A child may also bolster his sense of mastery by becoming absorbed in gadgets and particularly such activities as remotely-controlled toys, video games and computers. These are fascinating to most children, but they acquire a special meaning for the child who feels lacking in competence. For such a child social contacts are apt to be threatening because one can neither predict with confidence nor control the responses of the people with whom one has social interactions. Gadgets, however, are both controllable and entirely predictable if one applies the correct rules, and therefore gadgets enhance the child's sense of skill and mastery, and nurture his narcissism. Manufacturers of gadgets seem to know it well since the content of most such games emphasizes both power and skill.

Many children with neuropsychological impairments, such as various forms of learning disability, cannot cope effectively with the persistent narcissistic trauma. Some of them employ crude compensatory devices: they become egocentric, self-aggrandizing individuals, overly concerned with ambition and public image, intolerant of criticism and often insensitive to the nuances of interpersonal situations. Some investigators call such people "social fools". They manifest many features of narcissistic personality. Some of them, indeed, should be so classified, but others only appear to be such. Closer scrutiny shows that those "pseudo-narcissistic" personalities are capable of true loving relationships when the object does not constitute a threat, e.g., they may be warm and considerate toward children and become deeply attached to a child. Therefore, the difference between narcissistic over-concern and over-sensitivity, which are a reaction to severe or prolonged narcissistic injury, and between true narcissistic personality, lies in the quality of object relationships (Kernberg, 1975).

Other individuals do not attempt to compensate for the narcissistic injury generated by deviant development. Their negative self-representation is ego-syntonic, and they develop insecure, passive, dependent personalities, sometimes with masochistic or self-derogatory character traits.

It is common knowledge that, as defence mechanisms give way during analysis, the patient's anxiety becomes more intense. This applies also to those defensive structures, such as compensations and coping devices which protect the patient's narcissism. When defence mechanisms give way, the repressed, ego-alien wishes emerge. When protective mechanisms are eroded, the patient becomes exposed to the unmitigated impact of his negative, despised self-representation. This can be a deeply distressing experience, which may tax the therapist's skill and empathy. Understanding the roots of negative self-representation, both innate and environmental, may be of crucial importance in overcoming the crisis.

CHAPTER SIX

Developmental Deviations and the Progression of Developmental Stages

The onset, progress and the termination of each developmental stage depends on the convergence of two processes: maturation of the organism and stimulation by the environment. Maturational deviations, e.g., lack of synchronization between perceptual, motor and cognitive functions, will delay or distort a developmental stage in which those specific functions are involved. Moreover, a developmental deviation that affects the environment, i.e., influences parents' relationship to the child, will also affect a stage which depends on that relationship. The latter issue, i.e., the effect of developmental deviations on the parents, will be the subject of the next chapter; in this one we discuss the direct effects of innate characteristics and maturational deviations on the various developmental stages.

A. Infancy: the oral-symbiotic stage

Innate characteristics influence significantly the way an infant experiences his world and deals with it (Korner, 1971; Brazelton, 1973; Thomas & Chess, 1977). The first variable that needs to be considered is *state of arousal*. Customarily we distinguish six states: deep sleep, light sleep, dozing, quiet alertness, active alertness and crying (Brazelton, 1973). As far as we know quiet alertness is the optimal state in the newborn for receiving and processing environmental information. Active alertness becomes equally or more important as a result of maturation of motor organization, i.e., visual scanning and focussing, and intentional hand movements. If these two optimal states are lacking and extreme states, that is deep sleep and crying, predominate, the infant will have less opportunity to receive and process environmental stimulation and that, in turn, may have an unfavorable effect on cognitive development.

The next variable to consider is *cognitive organization*. Early cognition is manifested by recognition of familiar stimuli; this recognition is normally accompained by a positive, pleasurable affect (Papoušek & Papoušek, 1983). We say "normally", because recognition of a familiar percept which is associated with a painful memory, e.g., a pediatrician's office, will evoke distress, not pleasure. It is important to emphasize, however, that recognition of the familiar *in itself* is pleasurable (see Chapters Eleven and Twelve). Some familiar percepts, associated with the primary caregiver, e.g., the sight of mother's face, acquire additional significance because they become associated with gratification of needs. The result is an exclusive attachment to a set of familiar percepts, that is mother, and exclusion of the unfamiliar. Hence, the development of the symbiotic stage requires four conditions: a degree of cognitive organization, a capacity to experience satisfaction of needs, the availability of a stable primary caregiver, and an ability of that caregiver to empathize with and gratify the baby's needs. The first factor., i.e., cognitive ability depends on maturation of the central nervous system, the second, that is ability to enjoy need satisfaction, depends on general functioning of the infant's organism, and the last two on the environment. If any of these fail, the symbiotic stage will be disrupted. In more severe cases there will be a failure to establish a symbiosis, i.e., autism; more often the symbiosis develops, but is tainted with excessive frustration and rage and a failure to develop "basic trust" (Erikson, 1970).

We have mentioned that a caregiver has to be able to understand intuitively, empathically, the needs of the infant. Korner & Grobstein (1967) observed that newborn infants vary in the ability to convey their needs clearly. Therefore the effectiveness of maternal ministrations and the balance between gratification and frustration depend not only on mother's competence but also on an innate ability on the part of the newborn to "signal" his needs.

Another group of innate characteristics of infants concerns

varying reactions to stimuli. A novel stimulus evokes so-called "alerting response" and a repetition of identical stimuli results in suppression of alerting response, i.e., habituation. There are considerable differences in the capacity to habituate between different infants, but each individual infant shows a fairly consistent capacity to habituate to stimuli of diverse kind (Aleksandrowicz & Aleksandrowicz, 1976). An infant cannot remove himself from a continuous or aversive stimulus nor can he control the source of it. Therefore habituation is his only means of protection from unnecessary or distressful stimuli. An infant whose capacity to habituate is impaired, for instance due to barbituates or opiates administered during delivery (Aleksandrowicz & Aleksandrowicz, 1974; Brackbill, 1979) is at risk of becoming over-stimulated, excitable and exhausted, unless his caregivers protect him from excessive stimulation.

The degree of *sensitivity* to stimuli also varies. Mild stimuli usually evoke interest, while intense ones tend to be distressful. Hypersensitive infants have more adverse reactions and extreme hypersensitivity may lead to severe psychopathology (Bergman & Escalona, 1949). In contrast, infants who are hypo-reactive to stimuli and show little interest in their surroundings are at risk of relative sensory deprivation and delay in cognitive development, unless their deficiency is compensated for by active stimulation on the part of the caregivers. *Modulation of affect* also shows innate variability. The infant's mood may be predominantly positive or negative (Thomas & Chess, 1977), the threshold of arousal, i.e., proneness to crying, may be high or low, the infant may be easy or difficult to soothe, he may be "cuddly" or "non-cuddly" (Brazelton, 1973). All these variables provide the emotional background for the symbiotic relationship and influence its course. Schaeffer and Emerson (1964), for instance, demonstrated that "cuddly" infants tend to form a symbiotic attachment earlier than "non-cuddly" ones.

Infants differ in the spontaneous rhythm of bodily movements. Kestenberg, et al. (1971, 1977) have demonstrated the importance of the merging of caregiver's movements into the baby's spontaneous rhythm.

In conclusion, the establishment and the quality of the symbiotic relationship depend on a synchronization and fit of infant's innate characteristics and maturational processes on the one hand, with the mother's competence on the other hand. The resolution of the symbiotic stage is initiated by the "differentiation" and "practicing" sub-phases (Mahler et al., 1975). "Practicing" consists of exploring one's body, mother's body and the environment, and gradually organizing these percepts into self-boundary (Mahler and McDevitt, 1982) and into a representation of the primary love-object, i.e., mother. This process requires a further maturation of visual-motor coordination and of cognition; it is also facilitated by an active, vigorous disposition on the part of the infant. A deficiency of any of these functions is apt to delay the resolution of symbiosis and the onset of separation-individuation.

B. Separation-individuation and the emergence of autonomy

This stage is characterized by a spurt in motor development, i.e., gross and fine motor coordination, visual-motor coordination, locomotion and sphincter control, and later by development of language. A delay or impairment of these functions is bound to affect the emotional and interpersonal development at this stage. Mahler, et al. (1975, pp. 72–74) found that the exhilaration accompanying the second sub-phase of the separation-individuation process depends on free locomotion. They also observed an upsurge in asserting individuality during the month following the attainment of free locomotion. Our own observations of mothers and infants, as well as our clinical experience, lead us to believe that a delay in locomotion often delays the development of autonomy and facilitates dependence in later life. We have also observed that poorly developed spatial orientation may be related to dependence and separation anxiety. The following case may serve as an example:

Mr. Z., a lawyer in his early forties, developed a disabling anxiety accompanied by fears of myocardial infarction, with hypochondrial preoccupations. He requested repeated medical tests and cardiological consultations but they achieved, at best, only temporary reassurance and relief. The anxiety was more or less continuous, but the patient experienced also acute spells of severe anxiety accompanied by weakness, fear of fainting and, on a few occasions, paroxysmal tachycardia. Mr. Z's condition developed at a time when he was about to leave his father's law firm, after several years of a very difficult partnership, in order to set up a practice of his own. Mr. Z's personality was characterized by pronounced dependence. During his illness he could not separate from his wife for any length of time and insisted that she should stay within reach. Mr. Z. had already experienced a period of severe anxiety in his early twenties, which required a brief hospitalization in a psychiatric unit of a general hospital. While there, he had insisted on his mother staying at his bedside and holding his hand.

In one of the sessions we discussed Mr. Z's childhood. It transpired that he had a conspicuously defective sense of orientation. Even though his school had been only half a mile away from his home, he always walked along the same route out of fear of losing his way. During his military service he had attended an officers' training course. He did well in most of the subjects except orientation exercises, which were, in his own words, "a nightmare".

This is just one of a number of patients in whom we have observed excessive dependence and separation anxiety in conjunction with poor spatial orientation. The relation is probably reciprocal. A toddler whose spatial orientation is poor will be afraid to venture out and will maintain a closer physical and emotional contact with his mother. At the same time a child who is afraid to separate from his mother refrains from exploring the environment and has fewer opportunities to practice and enhance his sense of orientation. In other words, we are dealing with a synergistic effect of a developmental variable (spacial orientation) and an emotional variable (autonomy).

The timing of speech development is also critical. The ability to express wishes and later to verbalize feelings is a milestone of emotional development (A. Katan, 1961). Verbalization facilitates modulation of affects and containing of aggression. We distinguish the following developmental stage of aggressive discharge (see also Chapter Twelve).

(1) Global response, i.e., diffuse motor and autonomic discharge;

(2) Behavioral response, manifested by intentional motor activity (e.g., kicking an object, biting, throwing);

(3) Verbal release, i.e., expressing the angry affect or the aggressive wish in words;
(4) Cognitive working-through.

A delay in the development of any of the functions listed, i.e., intentional mobility, language, or ability to analyze conceptually, may interfere with the maturation of aggressive discharge.

C. The Oedipal stage

The Oedipal stage marks the development of affectionate object relationships, ambivalence and the beginning of sexual identity.

Those children in whom the symbiotic stage or the separation-individuation stage have not been successfully resolved will encounter difficulties in establishing affectionate object relationships in the Oedipal stage. To love another person one has to be able to perceive the object of love, cognitively and emotionally, as a separate person with his or her own feelings and needs. During pre-Oedipal stages of development the object is perceived as a part of oneself or merely as an all-powerful need-satisfying agency. The Oedipal child has also to learn to cope with ambivalence, i.e., love and hate directed at the same object. This requires a clear-cut differentiation of feelings, a characteristic which needs to mature. An infant's emotional states and affects are fluid, nebulous and poorly differentiated (Bridges, 1932), e.g., intense joy may easily turn into distress. In toddlers affectionate hugging and aggressive "grabbing" are not easily distinguished. The child in the Oedipal stage, however, shows a sharp delineation between affection and anger, and therefore he can be fully aware of his contradictory feelings. If the maturation process, that is a differentiation of positive and negative feelings, is delayed, there is a blurring rather than contradiction. Instead of an emotional conflict between love and hate, there is an infusion of affectionate relationships with aggression.

In conclusion, one of the main developmental objectives of the Oedipal stage is the establishment of ambivalent object relationships. This depends on two prerequisites: (a) There has to be a consolidated object representation, and (b) There has to be a clear-cut differentiation of affectionate and hostile impulses.

The pre-Oedipal child envies his parents' omnipotence, but the Oedipal child goes one step further and attempts to stand up to the parent and to compete. In order to embark on such a fearsome adventure the small child needs considerable self-assurance as well as trust in the parents' benevolence. At this point the feelings of competence and sense of body mastery acquired during the second year of life assist the child to rise to the Oedipal challenges. A developmental lag or impairment that interferes with the establishment of competence will often affect the child's ability to experience and express competitive, hostile wishes during the Oedipal stage. For instance, many children with slow or defective motor development fail to acquire the normal assertiveness of the Oedipal child and tend to regress to a clinging-dependent or passive-aggressive relationship with the parent of the same sex.

The next developmental objective of the Oedipal stage is the formation of early sexual identity, a gradual process which will continue throughout adolescence. The primary mechanism for the establishment of sexual identity is identification with the parent of the same sex, though other factors, such as perception of one's body and social reinforcements, also participate in the process.

The identification with the parent of the same sex may encounter difficulties when there is a significant temperamental incompatibility between the parent and the child. A chronic conflict between the two will *not* impede an identification, at most it may result in excessive aggression or guilt, but *estrangement* may well impede it. Temperamental affinity strengthens the *normal* narcissistic tie between parent and child, i.e., the parent's perception of the child as an extension of himself. Therefore, temperamental affinity makes it easier for the child to identify with the parent. As an example of such affinity we may quote the father who said: "I know when my daughter is up to mischief because I would have done the same were I in her place." If there is a strong temperamental affinity with the parent of the *opposite* sex the result may be ambiguity or con-

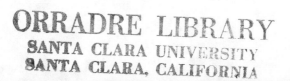

flict in the sexual identification. The greatest obstacle to identification, however, is a temperamental mismatch with the
parent of the same sex and the ensuing alienation, expressed
by statements like: "Is this my child?" or "I could never understand Johnny, from the time he was a baby. I would sometimes
get mad at the other kids, but Johnny I just couldn't figure
out." For a child who is a "biological stranger" (Aleksandrowicz, 1975a) to his parent, identification with that parent and
resolution of the Oedipal situation is arduous and fraught with
conflict. Parts of super-ego and ego-ideal are treated uncon-
sciously as internalized foreign bodies, imposed forcibly, alien
and hostile.

In conclusion, the successful outcome of the Oedipal stage
requires (a) firm object representations in order to direct affectionate and hostile feelings at them; (b) a differentiation of
affectionate and hostile feelings in order to experience emotional conflict and ambivalence; (c) a sense of competence to dare
to compete with the parents, and (d) enough temperamental
affinity with the parent to form ego-syntonic identification, and
lay the foundations for sexual identity and integrated ego-
ideals.

D. Latency: school age

Latency is characterized by a spurt in cognitive abilities, especially reality-oriented, "secondary" thinking and an expansion
of the social sphere, especially peer relationships. Developmental impairment may imperil both.

"Secondary", reality-oriented cognition develops slowly as
the young child becomes familiar with his environment and
learns to recognize its lawful properties. It never replaces
"primary" cognition entirely, though it later assumes a larger
role in directing behavior (Noy, 1969). During intrauterine existence the fetus finds himself in what may be called "primary
state": a condition of only minimal deviations from the optimal
balance of vital needs, with gentle, continuous tactile, auditory
and proprioceptive stimulation, which assures development
and maturation of psychic functions. Extrauterine existence
allows only limited opportunities for "primary state" and the

infant needs to supplement the mother's ministrations by self-consolatory measures, that is, by "primary" cognition, aimed at restoring, as far as possible, a condition approaching the "primary state". At first, "primary" cognition consists, as far as we can infer, of hallucinatory gratification. Later on, when cognitive processes become more structured, hallucinations are replaced by fantasies, day-dreams and wishful thinking.

Reality-oriented, "secondary" cognition develops in parallel to "primary" cognition, and its control over behavior shows a steep rise when the child moves from the Oedipal stage into latency.

A child's growing interest in reality and gradual relinquishing of fantasy is due to maturation of cognitive skills, but requires reinforcements. The awards that consolidate reality-oriented thinking and behavior consist of real gratification of (socially acceptable) wishes, social reinforcements, i.e., praise or status, and; last but not least, gratification of the need for mastery. Fantasy offers a wide choice of narcissistic gratifications, none of them, however, can compete with a real accomplishment. Growing up, we trade the omnipotence of fantasy for the fulfilment of mastery.

A child with a learning disability, impaired motor or visual-motor coordination, or any other neuropsychological impairment, grows up with an insecure competence; once he reaches latency he runs the risk of further damage to his competence because of difficulties encountered in school or in extra-curricular activities. The temptation is great then to withdraw into either private fantasies, i.e., day dreams, or "manufactured" fantasies, such as video or computer games. The content of the day dreams and fantasies of such children is almost invariably grandiose and aggressive, indicating their source: narcissistic injury, feelings of powerlessness and impotent rage. The withdrawal into fantasies detracts from the incentive to practice reality testing and social competence. The child tends to remain immature, self-centered and susceptible to instinctual needs.

Peer relationships of the child with developmental deviations may also be affected negatively by his poor academic or athletic achievements. Moreover, personality traits common in children with Attention Deficit Disorder constitute a social handicap:

short attention span, impulsivity and irritability, low frustration tolerance and, in some of them, unexpected lapses of social judgment, like saying the right thing at the wrong time. The child's low self-esteem causes social timidity or clumsy compensatory efforts which also do not help his peer relationships. In conclusion, the main developmental objectives of latency, i.e., emotional investment in learning, consolidation of reality-oriented thinking and behavior, and expansion of social interactions, are apt to be delayed or distorted by developmental deficiencies. The result may be inadequate social skills and a fixation of emotional investment on need-gratifying fantasy.

E. Adolescence

The main developmental objectives of adolescence are:

(a) To contain the rising tide of libidinal and aggressive drives and to direct them into adaptive and socially acceptable channels of discharge;
(b) To relinquish the original Oedipal love objects and to direct libido to peers;
(c) To consolidate sexual identity;
(d) To cope with the growing demands and responsibilities placed by the society, to "come of age".

(a) Containing and channelling of drives may become a very difficult task for children whose developmental deviation involves impairment of impulse control, for instance, most hyperkinetic children. Adolescence for them and their parents can be a trying and turbulent time, manifested by sexual promiscuity, running away, juvenile delinquency, or other forms of social maladjustment. It is important to determine whether the maladaptive behavior is an expression of a deep-seated personality disorder, a result of social factors, or a result of developmentally-determined impulsivity and poor judgment. The latter condition allows a more optimistic outlook, provided the environment can act with firmness, understanding and patience.

(b) Relinquishing the tie to parents involves overcoming dependence. Those children whose developmental deviation resulted in excessive dependence, e.g., some children with delayed motor development or impaired spatial orientation, will experience more than usual difficulty in separating from their infantile love objects.

(c) The formation of sexual identity during adolescence has its roots in the Oedipal stage. If the latter was less than successful, the process of consolidation during adolescence may also encounter difficulties.

(d) Coping with demands and assuming responsibilities requires a solid basis of reality-oriented, secondary thought processes and effective social skills. A youth who failed to acquire those resources during latency will find the demands of adolescence difficult to cope with. He may withdraw even more into the world of need-gratifying fantasy, or attempt desperately to gain acceptance and respect of the peer group by ill-conceived, impulseridden sexual or aggressive behavior, become "a rebel without a cause".

In conclusion, adolescence of children with developmental deviations can be a stormy, difficult and even dangerous time. It is important, however, to keep in mind that developmental deviations alone do not determine the form or severity of the problems. A great deal depends on environmental factors: home situation, educational facilities, peer group, and sublimatory outlets and supports available in the community. Therefore, understanding the nature of a developmental deviation is not enough in order to predict adolescent adaptation or lack of it with confidence.

In addition to the difficulties and distortions that affect each stage in children with developmental deviations there seems to be a non-specific factor that may interfere with the progression of all developmental stages. We refer to a certain rigidity of cognitive, emotional and behavioral patterns which one often notices in subjects with subtle neuropsychologic impairments. Different investigators describe children with Attention Deficit Disorder as "not amenable to educational methods", "unable to learn from experience" or "non-responsive to reinforcements". In our opinion, it would be more appropriate to refer to this quality as a lack of mobility, an inertia of established cognitive and emotional patterns. Freud, in his reference to "adhesiveness of the libido" and to "depletion of plasticity" (Freud, 1937a, pp. 241–242) was probably referring to the same phenomenon. For such a child, each transition from one developmental stage into the next one requires more time and more energy, therefore, he also needs more help and more patience on the part of the caregivers.

In summary, each developmental stage requires the simultaneous maturation of specific perceptual, motor and cognitive functions in order to usher, develop and terminate that stage (see Chapter Twelve). Some functions compel the child to enter a particular stage, i.e., perceptual and cognitive maturation make the separation of self and non-self unavoidable. Other functions provide the means and the gratifications needed to work through the processes involved. For instance, motor maturation provides the means to struggle through the process of separation-individuation and the opportunity to release aggression which is also a critical component of separation-individuation (McDevitt, 1983). Termination of a stage is also facilitated by maturation, i.e., the blossoming of physical and cognitive faculties that occurs at the beginning of latency facilitating the termination of the Oedipal stage and a shift of libidal investment onto the exciting wide world of middle childhood.

Last, not least, the transition from one developmental stage to the next requires a flexibility of emotional and behavioral patterns. Hence, a rich spectrum of individual innate characteristics and the variability of the maturational timetable interact with environmental factors to determine the progression of developmental stages.

CHAPTER SEVEN

The Effect of Developmental Deviations on Parents

The impact of a child's developmental deviation on his parents depends on a number of factors:

(a) The nature of the deviation, i.e., the child's age, the areas of functioning that are affected and the severity of the developmental delay or impairment;

(b) The parents' personalities, i.e. their own unresolved emotional conflicts as well as their intellectual and emotional resources. Can they understand the nature of the problem and its ramifications? Can they empathize with the "different" child? Can they tolerate their own ambivalence? What are their hopes and expectations from the child and can they re-assess them?

(c) The social setting, i.e. cultural norms and expectations as well as the availability and effectiveness of support systems, such as extended family, community services and professional agencies.

In this chapter we examine the impact of various deviations from infancy till latency. The role of parents' personality and of support systems will be discussed in the context of counselling for parents (Chapter Nine).

Every infant shapes his or her parents' caregiving behavior from the moment of birth; he does so by responding or failing to respond to the caregiver's intuitive ways of ministering to his needs. Parents learn from each child how to feed, to comfort, to play with *him*. What may appear to an uninformed observer as incompetent parenting may well be an appropriate response to a developmentally deviant infant; a response that was developed intuitively or learned from bitter experience.

Therefore, assessing the caregiving skills of a parent of a developmentally deviant infant or child, requires careful observation and prudence in passing judgment. Comforting an infant in distress is one of the critical caregiving skills. Normal infants can often be comforted by exposing them to stimuli that evoke interest, e.g. holding the baby propped up against the caregiver's shoulder in order to expose him to a wide visual field, talking to the child, or offering an interesting object to examine. Restless, irritable infants that cannot be soothed by perceptual stimulation may condition the parents to use other means, such as frequent feedings, to cope with the infant's distress. Such a comforting technique may prove temporarily effective, albeit at the price of interfering with the child's natural hunger-satiation cycle and perhaps with his sleep-cycle as well. It also engenders the risk of an excessively strong tie between feeding and comfort.

In other words, undesirable child-handling methods may develop as a council of despair, not necessarily as a result of deep-rooted neurotic aberrations in the parents.

The following example illustrates a "desperate" comforting technique and its results (Aleksandrowicz & Aleksandrowicz, 1975b):

> Carmel was a wanted child. Her mother had one normal pregnancy nine years previously, followed by a miscarriage and a prolonged infertility. The second pregnancy was normal, but the delivery was one month overdue. During Carmel's delivery the mother was heavily medicated including oxytocin, meperidine and inhalation anaesthesia. The child appeared healthy and her physical development was normal. Neonatal Behavioral Assessment Scale (Brazelton, 1973) was administered, as part of a research project, daily during the first five days of life, and then on days 7, 10 and 28. Carmel showed consistently high scores on items related to "excitability" and high "habituation" scores, i.e. she cried easily or "ignored" repeated stimuli and went to sleep. Her responsiveness to visual and auditory stimuli was consistently low; her "cuddliness" score and number of spontaneous smiles diminished over the 28 days of testing. Carmel was followed-up by home visits for two years. As an infant she was extremely difficult to care for: fussy, irritable and crying inconsolably. She reacted negatively to most novel stimuli (Thomas & Chess, 1977) and developed an intense fear of anyone outside her immediate family.
> Carmel's mother used feeding as the principal soothing method. By the time father returned from his work mother was usually exhausted

and eager to turn the baby over to the father, and Carmel and her father established over the first year a very close relationship, albeit a somewhat peculiar one. Father would walk for hours holding Carmel in his arms, talking to her affectionately and rocking her. When that did not soothe her he would turn around, jump up and down and toss the baby till she stopped crying and fell into an exhausted sleep. In other words this most unusual and questionable handling method achieved its aim. Mother described it by saying: "Daddy had his way with Carmel; she is really Daddy's daughter." While this went on mother would watch impassively and Carmel's older brother was shut-off from the action and, in general, discouraged by his parents from taking care of the baby.

At the age of two-and-a-half Carmel's motor and cognitive development were normal. Her social and emotional development, however, was seriously impaired. She was a withdrawn, insecure child, clinging to her father most of the time. Carmel showed minimal interest in toys, would not play by herself, and responded distrustfully and hesitantly to other children's social overtures. Her parents reported that she could be left with her regular baby-sister, or maternal grandmother, but otherwise showed intractable stranger anxiety.

In conclusion, Carmel's impaired social and emotional development seems to have been due to an excessively intense and exclusive attachment to her father, (and her mother to a lesser extent) which delayed the process of separation-individuation. This pathological attachment, however, was rooted in father's maladroit efforts to cope with an extremely difficult infant, of a type that Thomas refers to as "mother killers" (Thomas et al., 1968). Feeding or prolonged body contact, accompanied by vigorous motion proved effective in soothing the child and therefore those two became firmly established methods of handling. In other words, the child's pathological responses shaped parental inappropriate handling techniques by a process of contingent conditioning. Those inappropriate handling methods in turn caused, or at least facilitated, gross impairment of emotional and social development. Parents learn from their baby how to be caregivers; in this case Carmel taught her father and mother how to be pathogenic parents.

Parents (or other caregivers) of a "difficult" infant have to learn also how to cope with excessive anxiety. A child's cry of distress is his primary mode of communication; it is intended to mobilize the adult's anxiety and it invariably does. An irritable, inconsolable, "difficult" infant generates anxiety far in excess of what we may call "normal" parenting anxiety. Not only is the caregiver's anxiety excessive in intensity; it is also unrelieved, seemingly interminable. Carmel's case illustrates how some parents cope; whatever the comforting method adopted, most families reach the stage where the entire household becomes organized around the needs of the "difficult" infant: subdued noise to avoid waking up the "tyrant", sleepless nights of rocking and walking, and ceaseless concern, at the expense of emotional supplies available to older siblings. Well-intentioned advice given to the mother, such as: "Try to relax, don't be so anxious and the baby will be all right" makes matters worse, by implying that it is the mother's anxiety that makes the baby difficult to cope with and not the other way round. Such uninformed counselling increases guilt and undermines even more mother's shaky self-confidence.

Some parents cannot control their aggression and either reject the child or abuse him physically. These cases require more extensive help. Even in less extreme cases the self-perpetuating cycle of failure to cope—anger—guilt—further failure—more anger—more guilt, leads to a grossly disturbed parent-child relationship. A common outcome is a sado-masochistic relationship in which the child learns to find an outlet for his own anger and guilt by manipulating the parent into more and more hostile attacks, sometimes tinged with erotic excitement.

In conclusion: developmental deviations during early infancy tend to undermine the positive, mutually gratifying aspect of caregiving. For that reason they pose a threat to early parent-child bond and imbue the symbiotic relationship with negative affect, i.e. rage and anxiety.

From the second half of the first year on the dialogue between the infant and his caregiver extends rapidly beyond physical and emotional needs. As the child takes an increasingly active interest in his surrounding and learns to manipulate objects, the caregiver assumes more and more the role of a "mediator" (Feuerstein, 1979) and teacher. Much of the time spent together is focused now on practicing and developing motor and cognitive skills. The caregiver's "mediation" consists of providing new sources of stimulation, suggesting "games" (e.g. switching the light, rattling a toy), and demostrating or "shaping" skills (e.g. pushing an object through an opening). Parental "mediation" involves also promoting the child's cognitive organization by providing so called "categorizing criteria". A caregiver conveys such "categorizing criteria" sometimes intentionally, in order to teach the child, and sometimes spontaneously, by exposing the child to the organized aspects of the adults' own lives. For instance, the parents teach the child to put all the toys into the toy box and all the pots on the shelf. They will also associate the object, its picture and its name, e.g. by pointing to a real cat and then a picture of a cat and saying "cat". Ordering objects into categories is the first level of abstract thinking.

The parent also "mirrors" the child's newly acquired skills by showing pleasure and approval when the child exhibits his accomplishments. Thus the parent becomes an active associate in the child's rapidly growing mastery and his "love affair with the world" (Mahler et al., 1975). This shared sense of growth and accomplishment is an emotionally rich experience with deep psychological roots.

Parents assume the role of a "mediator" intuitively in response to cues from the infant. We all seem to be "pre-programmed" to act as teachers of infants and children, even though more and more parents nowadays make also a deliberate effort to enrich their child and to stimulate cognitive growth. Koestler et al. (1987) suggested that adults have an innate need to impart skills just as children have an innate need to acquire them.

In Chapter Four we have suggested that the positive affect associated with acquiring and exercising skills helps to consolidate the self. Now we suggest that the pleasure the child derives from acquiring cognitive and motor skills with the "mediator's" assistance, helps to consolidate the infant-parent bond. The child not only learns willingly from his parents because he loves them; he also loves his parents because they teach him (Chapter Eleven).

Developmental deviations that interfere with the acquisition of new skills, e.g. delay of speech, attention deficit, poor motor co-ordination or behavioral rigidity (see Chapter Three), interfere inevitably with the emotional bond generated by teaching. The parent becomes just as frustrated by the child's ineffectual performance, as the child is. The failure of interaction undermines the parent's confidence in *his*, or her, parenting ability. It generates anxiety, narcissistic injury, anger and guilt. Some parents blame themselves and invent ingenious psychodynamic explanations to spare themselves and the child the narcissistic injury of admitting an innate "defect". Others blame the

child: "She trips on air," "He is just stubborn and won't do it."
Many parents withdraw emotionally from "mediated" teaching
and provide basic physical, perhaps also emotional needs, but
refrain from engaging the child in shared activities. Such withdrawal, coupled with the child's natural inclination to avoid
frustrating activities, tends to aggravate the deficit because of
lack of practice. As the child grows older some developmental
lags are left behind, but other difficulties appear, because the
child's world expands and the demands of the society become
more complex. The child and the parents now compare his
performance to that of his peers and the narcissistic injury
deepens. The child with poor visual-motor coordination cannot
draw, the clumsy one cannot run fast or catch the ball. The
restless child cannot sit while the teacher reads a story, the
impulsive one gets into trouble, and the child with poor retention memory cannot remember what the teacher just said. The
parents have to contain not only their child's misery and helpless anger, but also the complaints and criticisms by teachers,
relatives and neighbors. Many parents begin now to develop
fantasies that the child is "defective", "retarded" or "crazy".
Such fears are reinforced by the child's unpredictable and
sometimes incomprehensible behavior: violent emotional reactions, or misunderstanding of instructions and misinterpreting
social situations due to concrete or literal thinking.

> Rick was a ten-year old boy seen in consultation because of a learning
> disability. The physician examined the child's gross motor co-ordination
> and dominance and told him: "That will be all, you may now sit down."
> Rick took the instruction literally and sat down where he was, without
> returning to his seat. Rick's mother blushed and apologized with embar-
> assment for the boy's maladroit behavior.
> Another child, asked whether he was attending a "small" (meaning
> special education) or a "large" (i.e. regular) class, answered: "It has four
> windows".

Such concrete, literal thinking sounds insane to the uninformed observer. Parents now begin to search for anything to
lay the blame on: heredity (usually that of the spouse), mis-
management of pregnancy, "emotional deprivation" in infancy
or anything else. Some parents attempt to minimize the problem by emphasizing the child's abilities and colluding with his

avoidance of tasks that he finds difficult. Others become over-protective and try to set up an environment that will not frustrate the child; they spare his feelings but delay his emotional growth and foster excessive dependence. Some parents resort to denial and praise what is patently an inadequate performance (e.g. a coarse scribble becomes a "beautiful drawing") thus increasing the child's confusion and undermining his trust in the adults.

In some families there is a split or division of roles. One parent, usually but not invariably the father, represents denial such as: "There is nothing wrong with the boy that a little firm discipline won't cure," while the other parent takes upon herself, or himself as the case may be, all the anxieties, frightening fantasies and pain. Acrimonious arguments often result, even though each parent may be partly right.

Even a more serious situation develops when one parent or both form a persecutory idea that a teacher, a counsellor or some other external agent is the sole cause of the child's present and future problems. We have seen, however, that even such extreme, grossly pathological attitudes, may respond to a frank sympathetic discussion of the child's impairment and a patient, supportive program of counselling and therapy. This indicates that what appears to be a sign of gross psychopathology in the parent may be only an irriational, desperate way of coping with an intolerably painful situation created by a developmentally impaired child.

In conclusion, deviant development in the child turns parenthood into a strenuous, frustrating and often ungrateful task. It is fraught with anxiety, anger, guilt and narcissistic hurt. It often cannot be accomplished without professional help. Yet children do improve with parents' efforts and persistence. Overcoming some of the obstacles and challenges described may in the long run give the parents a deep and well-earned satisfaction of having accomplished what seemed at the time a mission impossible.

CHAPTER EIGHT
_____

Treatment Strategies: The Role of Psychotherapy and the Analysis of Adaptive Ego Functions

In this chapter we examine the implications of the study of developmental deviations for psychoanalysis and dynamic psychotherapy. Developmental deviations, i.e., idiosyncratic temperament and subtle neuropsychological deficits, are common (Small, 1973). Children with neuropsychological impairments constitute a high proportion of maladjusted children (Rubin et al., 1972) and it is reasonable to assume that developmental deviations will be found to be a contributing factor to the personality formation in a significant number of patients referred to psychoanalysis or psychotherapy. Can psychoanalysis or dynamic psychotherapy help them? What are the indications for psychotherapy versus other treatments? Do developmental deviations require modifications of psychoanalytic technique and do they impose a limit on the objectives of treatment? The answers to these questions depend on the type and severity of the disturbance as well as on the age of the patient; we will formulate some general guidelines and present clinical illustrations.

In younger children with developmental deviations, counselling parents is an essential and often sufficient treatment strategy (Chapter Nine). In older children, adolescents and adults psychotherapy or psychoanalysis may be indicated.

A. The place of psychotherapy among treatment options

Subjects with emotional problems related to developmental deviations can be helped by interventions that achieve one or more of the following objectives:

(a) An improvement of the impaired function;
(b) An improvement in the overall functioning in spite of the specific disability;
(c) Opportunities for adaptive discharge of drives, e.g., outlets for aggression or narcissistic gratifications;
(d) Reduction of the emotional effects of the deviation, especially low self-esteem, anxiety or depression (Chapter Four).

We may illustrate the issue of treatment choice by means of a hypothetical but common clinical case. An adolescent boy is referred because of underachievement, social isolation, poor peer relationships and depressed moods. A diagnostic assessment shows Attention Deficit Disorder, which is not reflected by gross academic failure because of the boy's exceptionally high intelligence. The patient is restless, but slow and clumsy, and his gross motor coordination is poor. He is also anhedonic, self-depreciating, with very low self-esteem, feels unloved and criticized by his parents.

A number of therapeutic approaches can be suggested and each will probably help to some extent. The educational program can be tailored to reduce frustration and provide opportunities for the youngster's remarkable analytic abilities. For instance, excelling in an elective course in computer programming or advanced mathematics will enhance self-esteem. A karate class will release pent-up aggression and enhance his neglected motor skills. Such extracurricular activities will also provide opportunity for social ties based on common interests. Stimulant or antidepressive medication may also be considered.

Any combination of such interventions will probably be beneficial, perhaps even sufficient to meet the therapeutic expectations of the patient and his family. Should one also advise psychotherapy? The decision, in this case, depends on treatment goals. Dynamic psychotherapy, if successful, will achieve all of the objectives mentioned above, but will also have an integrative effect that the auxiliary therapies or environmental manipulations do not have. Dynamic psychotherapy and psychoanalysis provide an understanding of one's personality make-up, unexpressed wishes, aspirations, disappointments and fears. Our hypothetical patient will be able to re-examine his view of himself, to reach a realistic assessment of his disabilities and of his talents. He will be able to see the relationship between his disabilities and disappointment with his performance on the one hand, and his low self-esteem, social timidity and underachievement on the other. He will have an opportunity to reassess his view of the parents. Do they really love him less? Or perhaps they are merely disappointed by his self-defeating behavior? Or maybe none of this is true and he merely projects on his parents the low opinion he has of himself? Only insight can bring together conflicting emotions, irrational cognitive sets and maladaptive behavior patterns. The result is an improved integration of the self, i.e., self-understanding and self-acceptance, that not only helps the patient to overcome his present difficulties, but equips him with the tools to cope more effectively with future stresses and challenges. In conclusion, a rational program of auxiliary interventions can resolve main symptoms and improve functioning greatly; psychotherapy or psychoanalysis can, in addition to functional improvement, also help to integrate the patient's personality.

Dynamic psychotherapy or psychoanalysis are indicated whenever the symptoms suggest a more extensive disturbance of personality structure, which goes beyond the direct effects of the developmental problem. A patient suffering from pervasive phobias or hysterical personality with masochistic trends will benefit very little from auxiliary interventions, even if we come to the conclusion that developmental deviations had a crucial part in the genesis of the neurosis. Psychoanalysis or psychotherapy are indicated in such cases, as much as in other neurotic patients, in whom no significant innate, developmental factors can be found.

B. Parameters of technique: analysis of adaptive ego functions

Once we accept the notion that innate developmental idiosyncrasies or impairments may play a significant role in shaping a patient's personality structure and symptoms, and we reach the conclusion that the patient needs psychoanalysis, we have to ascertain that *such innate factors come to light and become integrated into the process of analysis,* as much as all other pathogenic influences. In other words, the basic psychoanalytic procedures, namely analysis of transference, analysis of defences and reconstruction, have to be supplemented by what we call "analysis of adaptive ego functions". We use the term "adaptive" as opposed to "defensive" ego functions, i.e., defence mechanisms. The primary task of the defence mechanisms is to ward off drives and to deal with intra-psychic conflicts. Defence mechanisms fulfill, to a certain extent, an adaptive purpose, but this is an indirect and secondary effect.

Adaptive ego functions, in contrast to defence mechanisms, are directed at the organism's environment and their primary and direct objective is to cope with it. They comprise perception, motility, cognition and so-called meta-cognitive, or integrative functions, such as reality judgment, decision making, planning, self-monitoring, and integrating cognitive and emotional processes. Adaptive functions may acquire a defensive role, i.e., in the process of conversion, motility or inhibition or motility may serve to ward off a forbidden wish, or spoken language may acquire the significance of anal discharge. These, however, are *secondary* roles, set up by "borrowing" a function from another realm. The boundary between adaptive and defensive functions may be flexible, but the essential difference is clear.

Obtaining information about the developmental deviation is the first step in the treatment of patients affected by it. A detailed developmental history and clinical examination will provide useful data. Certain relatively common symptoms ought to attract attention to the possibility of developmental factors being involved. These include uneven school performance (e.g., mediocre in elementary school, brilliant in college), strikingly low self-esteem, underachievement at work, and self-defeating life style. Propensity to anxiety, affective lability or impairment of impulse control should likewise attract attention to the possibility of developmental factors being present. Two clinical vignettes will serve as examples.

Evelyn D., a 21-year-old single college student, was seen at the request of her mother. Mrs. D. complained that Evelyn was childish, excessively dependent and clinging. Mrs. D. was particularly annoyed at Evelyn's habit of involving the mother in her, that is Evelyn's, personal problems and difficulties, and then criticizing the mother angrily for being "bossy" and "intruding".

During the initial visit, Evelyn, a bright, attractive young woman, appeared frank, co-operative and motivated, conveying a sense of warmth and trust. She had many critical complaints about herself, such as being impulsive, saying and doing things she regretted, "never counting to ten". Her major source of unhappiness, however, was related to her intellectual performance. Though obviously endowed with high intelligence, she had reading difficulties in the first grade, which she overcame with the help of her father. She always saw herself as the "dumb" member of the family, while her gifted father and brother were "geniuses". Her handwriting was illegible and she made spelling mistakes. Her work record was uneven: she failed to qualify for a junior managerial position, but then did exceptionally well as a P.R. officer in a government agency. While doing fairly well in her college language studies, she had to give up hopes of becoming a simultaneous translator because she could never recall the text. Poor memory, in fact, was Evelyn's most painful symptom. For instance, she found herself unable to discuss, during a social gathering, a popular novel which she had read a few months previously. She no longer remembered what the book was about. At times she thought in desperation that hers was a case of a "juvenile Alzheimer's disease" and such thoughts made her want to commit suicide. Clinical psychological tests revealed circumscribed neuropsychological impairments. There was a wide inter-test scatter in WAIS: from a score of 7 on Information, reflecting memory problems and avoidance of reading, to a striking score of 18 on Comprehension. Visual memory was excellent: a score of 17 in Digit Symbol and a recall of 8 forms in Bender Gestalt. Evelyn also achieved a good score on Digit Span by visualizing the figures on the windowpane as the examiner read them and then "reading" them from the window.

Difficulties in integrating perceptual fields were seen in Block Design and Picture Arrangement. DAP and Bender Test indicated a moderate impairment of visual-motor coordination, and a tendency to persevere. The Rorschach protocol was unusual and complex. It showed a rich creative imagination, i.e., positive original answers, and a basically solid reality judgment reflected in many popular answers. Yet many of those adequate percepts were tainted by inappropriate additional comments, which could lead one to score them as F- responses. That seemed to be related to anxiety, intellectual competitiveness, and, at times, to an inability to cope with several simultaneous stimuli. There were a few C/F answers and no other color responses, an indication of a difficulty to integrate emotional stimuli into cognitive processes. In conclusion, it was felt that Evelyn's emotional immaturity and instability, her narcissistic vulnerability and childish, adolescent-like attachment to mother, could be described as the effect of circumscribed, but significant neurop-sychological impairments in a very bright girl, who grew up in a warm, but intellectually demanding, achievement-oriented atmosphere. It was felt that Evelyn did not require extensive therapy, even though she had the potential to use one; informed counselling and a brief expressive therapy were recommended.

The case that follows illustrates the emergence of subtle neuro-psychological problems during the examination of a patient with an atypical clinical picture:

Mrs. T., a school-teacher and mother of four, was referred for psychiat-ric consultation by her counsellor because of long-standing recurrent depressive moods. She was reserved and diffident, obviously uncom-fortable about seeing a psychiatrist and her complaints were vague. She described herself as having "ups and downs": These were fluctuating moods rather than true depressive states. She also descibed "highs", that is, states of heightened energy and activity. She did not feel elated during these "highs". To the contrary, she felt distinctly uncomfortable and often anxious. Both the "highs" and the "downs", i.e., feelings of discouragement and listlessness, were clearly related to life events, that is, satisfactions and disappointments, even very minor ones.

Mrs. T. reported that her symptoms began at the age of fourteen. While in college she was briefly in treatment at a student mental health service but she "ran away from it". Mrs. T. was vague in describing her past as much as in describing her symptoms. She complained that her memory was poor: She could not recall what she said or where she put her things. On questioning she described other minor difficulties: She could not draw except crude "stick figures", her visual-motor coordina-tion was very poor ("My husband does all the sewing") and she was partially ambidextrous. Her spatial orientation was grossly inadequate and so was her right-left discrimination. Finding her way in an unfamil-iar place was totally impossible.

The psychiatrist tried to explain the meaning of her difficulties to the patient, and asked her: "Being a teacher you probably know about so-called learning disabilities?" Mrs. T. replied: "Yes, my two boys are dyslectic".

At this point of the interview, Mrs. T. appeared more relaxed and less diffident. She still objected to any kind of medication, but suggested she might benefit from psychotherapy, apparently sensing that the psychiat-rist understood her better than she expected. Mrs. T. explained that her depressive moods did not disturb her so much as her insecurity and exaggerated sensitivity to criticism or disappointment. Rather unex-pectedly she added: "I am also afraid of myself".

This brief interview, though by no means an exhaustive diagnostic study, provided presumptive evidence that neuropsychological impair-

ments, perhaps of a familial type, played a major role in Mrs. T.'s
personality formation and adjustment difficulties.

The study of neuropsychological impairments and temperamental idiosyndrasies does not end with the diagnostic
assessment but continues through-out analysis. Descriptions
of problems that the patient encounters at work, school or in
everyday life provide a wealth of information.

> Mrs. J., whose case has been referred to before, experienced difficulties
> in attending to several stimuli at the same time or experiencing an affect
> and attending to an unrelated task. She reported the following event: "I
> was talking to a friend who was accompanied by her little daughter. The
> child tried to attract her mother's attention; my friend would smile to the
> child, say a few words, and then return to our conversation. I suddenly
> envied her, as I realized that I could never do such a thing, that is, to
> smile to one person and have a serious conversation with another." This
> was just one of many examples of a deficiency in "shifting" described by
> this highly intelligent and perceptive woman.

A patient's behavior during the session itself is also a valu-
able source of information about adaptive functions, such as
memory, and ability to organize concepts or to abstract. The
response to interpretations depends not only on the degree of
resistance but also on the ability to shift from one cognitive set
to another, i.e., organize the same data according to a new
conceptual structure. Temperamental qualities, such as degree
of activity or tempo of cognition, can also be observed in
analytic sessions.

Last, not least, temperamental characteristics are manifested
with great intensity in the transference. It seems that the regression that takes place in the transferential relationship
brings forth the childhood temperamental characteristics in a
highly intensified form, a factor that can contribute to analytic
reconstruction. This will be discussed in Chapter Eleven.

We will now present the case of Mrs. J. in more detail, in
order to demonstrate how analysis of and insight into adaptive
functions can be integrated into the process of psychoanalysis.

> Mrs. J. was a married woman in her early thirties, a mother of three
> children, who was referred to analysis because two years of supportive
> therapy failed to produce any improvement. She was suffering from

severe phobias, and particularly from fear of committing suicide impulsively. She could not stand near a street or highway or enter high-rise buildings. There were other phobias, too: she was afraid of crowded or closed spaces, could not eat in a restaurant nor travel on a bus. Her range of activities had become extremely limited and she had to be accompanied by her husband everywhere, including therapy.

This disabling illness developed about three years earlier following two traumatic events: (a) Mrs. J. had quarrelled with her mother and asked her not to visit anymore, and (b) Mr. J., her husband, had a fainting spell after donating blood and the patient became afraid that he might die.

Mrs. J. was a bright, perceptive woman with considerable gifts for observation and a willingness to understand herself. Nevertheless, the decision to commence analysis was taken with uneasiness because of reservations about the severity of her disturbance. Mrs. J. appeared to be very self-centered, with hardly any significant object relationship, apart from an intense, unbridled, possessive attachment to her children. Her narcissistic vulnerability, raw, undisguised envy and diffidence indicated a primitive, instinct-ridden personality structure. The psychological test report described her as "borderline personality", especially because of pathological results of the Rorschach test. There were many answers, some of them imaginative and creative but also many inadequate percepts (F+ 58%) and relatively many unmodulated emotional responses (2C, 4CF, 3FC).

The decision to treat the patient by analysis was based on the clinical impression of strong motivation, ability to observe and reflect, as well as the patient's ability to function relatively well before the present illness. Mrs. J. was the older of two children born in a very disturbed home. Her father, a highly capable engineer and industrialist, was absorbed in his work, insensitive to his family's material and emotional needs, given to violent temper outbursts and abusive to the patient. The mother, an embittered, angry woman, felt rejected and unjustly treated by fate, by her parents and her husband. She threatened suicide on many occasions and Mrs. J., her confidante and only support, would miss school and keep watch over the mother. When Mrs. J. was twelve years old the mother sent Mrs. J. to buy cigarettes and, when left alone, slashed her wrists. She had to be hospitalized for several days and Mrs. J. was left with a deeply traumatic memory.

Mrs. J. left home when she was eighteen. Soon after she married a man for whom she had little affection and no respect. Her parents moved to another country, divorced a few years later and visited her infrequently. The reason for Mrs. J.'s turning finally against the mother was the latter's selfish, demanding behavior during one of those visits and her callous indifference to the grandchildren.

It was not difficult for the analyst to see that Mrs. J.'s phobias represented her fear of aggressive, murderous impulses against the mother and a guilty identification with mother's suicidal wishes. That interpretation, however, had very little effect on the patient. She could barely comprehend it intellectually; emotionally it meant nothing. Mrs. J. was in the grip of terrifying thoughts about losing her mind, about being submerged by affects and driven by uncontrollable impulses. Gradually it emerged that the patient, though outwardly inhibited, was in fact an intensely impulsive person, prone to emotional, irrational reactions, that she could not always control. She was easily overcome by anger, sadness or elation and her social judgment was not always sound. In other words, her fears of being out of control or losing her sanity, although grossly exaggerated, were not without some foundation in reality. It transpired gradually that Mrs. J.'s impulsiveness and affective "flooding" were part of a more generalized neuropsychological impairment, consisting of short attention span, inability to attend to several stimuli simultaneously, difficulties in "shifting" cognitive or affective set (see Ch. III), impaired motor coordination, and right-left discrimination, mixed dominance (right eye, left hand), and poor retention memory.

The results of the Rorschach test could now be re-interpreted considering the clinical evidence of subtle, but pervasive neuropsychological impairment, rich visual imagination, with uneven reality judgment and unmodulated, labile affect. The pathogenesis could be assumed to be a combination of innate impairment and a highly unfavorable home environment, characterized by lack of empathy, instability and unrestrained expressions of aggression.

At this point in treatment we embarked on a systematic examination of Mrs. J.'s impaired ego functions and their emotional implications: insecurity, lack of trust in her sanity or critical ability, poor self-esteem, and a need to please and to depend on others to provide ego functions in which she felt deficient, such as control of drives.

At the same time we explored dynamic factors: her hostile dependence on the husband, possessive love of the children, deep hatred and fear of her father along with a repressed longing for his love. One could describe the course of analysis as a pendulum motion: no sooner would we work through a neuropsychological problem and its emotional impact when a dynamic issue would appear, and vice versa. It was only when the issues of impulse control and fear of insanity had been extensively worked through that Mrs. J. found the courage to confront her repressed, murderous hate for her mother. With that the fears of suicidal impulses were resolved completely. At this stage of treatment the patient was free to move about, driving her car to therapy and even went on a trip abroad. She found work, first as a saleswoman and later as floor manager and buyer in a clothing store, and finally as a personal secretary to a company manager.

The case of Mrs. J. illustrates the technique we apply to patients with developmental idiosyncrasies and impairments. We study those personality traits and functional weaknesses carefully and present to the patient our tentative interpreta-

tions of their emotional impact. We interpret the effect of
deviations on self-representation, especially on the patient's
sense of competence and self-esteem, on the early relationships
with the parents, on the current object relationships and on
transference. We also interpret how innate qualities are used
defensively, e.g., passivity to disguise aggression, or to control
another person. In this way the analysis of adaptive ego functions and the analysis of conflicts and defenses not only
proceed simultaneously, but the reciprocal, inter-connecting
threads are also explored.

C. Goals and limits of psychotherapy and psychoanalysis

Some of the patients with developmental deviations and
neuropsychological impairment develop a clinical picture so
severe as to preclude exploratory psychotherapy or psychoanalysis. Even in such a case, however, insight into the developmental factors helps supportive therapy and rehabilitation.

In patients for whom analysis is indicated there may be some
limitations to therapeutic goals. The neuropsychological deficit
does not disappear; the patient learns to cope with it, and,
more importantly, to accept it as part of his self. That, indeed,
is one of the major therapeutic objectives: to bring to light the
patient's *real* assets and liabilities and his or her natural inclinations, to accept them and thus to consolidate a more
stable, better integrated self.

Another limitation may be an innate lack of flexibility, the
"psychic inertia" or "moving in loops" described in Chapter
Three. This inertia has been mentioned by Freud (1973a) as an
obstacles to analysis. In some of our patients it may not have
prevented achieving good therapeutic results, but caused the
process to be slow and prolonged.

A more serious difficulty was encountered in the case of Mr.
Y. (see Chapter Three). His poor attention span and seriously
impaired sequential auditory memory interfered with continuity of treatment. At times it seemed like writing on water, even
when the patient's motivation was positive and his negativism

at an ebb. Worse still, the lack of memory continuity seemed to be paralleled by an internal inability to integrate, to experience the past, the present and the transference within an integrated Gestalt. Such an integration, simultaneously cognitive and affective, is the core of psychoanalytic treatment. In this case it failed to appear, and the patient's insights remained compartmentalized and isolated. Mr. Y. derived considerable symptomatic benefit from treatment, but a basic change in personality appeared to be beyond his reach.

Some patients have great difficulty in accepting their limitations and reassessing their ego-ideals in a manner consonant with their temperament and inclinations, rather than reflecting parental ideals and expectations. Interpretation and working-through are sufficient to free some analysands from internalized parental authority, but others need also a measure of benevolent support. The same applies to self-esteem. For some patients an interpretation of the narcissistic injury and the compensatory mechanisms is enough, while others need a certain amount of support before a healthy narcissism is consolidated.

Confronting the devices that protect the patient from narcissistic injury requires prudence. Just as confrontation of a neurotic defence, e.g., a well-timed interpretation, is apt to increase anxiety, so interpretation of a narcissistic coping device may result in depression. To reduce that danger the analyst has to depend on the therapeutic alliance and trust generated by understanding and explaining to the patient his functional impairments.

Last, not least, there seems to be a limit to the extent that the late effects of the damage caused by a developmental deviation to the early mother-child relationship can be undone. In some patients we have observed a sense of being unloved and a sensitivity to rejection so deeply ingrained that no amount of insight acquired in analysis could resolve it entirely, even though it could moderate its intensity and influence.

In conclusion, many patients whose emotional difficulties and maladaptive behavior stem from developmental deviations can and should be treated by psychoanalysis or dynamic psychotherapy. The following conditions will facilitate a therapeutic success in such patients:

(a) One needs a clear understanding of the developmental deviation, its impact on the patient's emotional life and on the development of object relationships;
(b) One has to integrate that information into the analytic process, i.e., analyze adaptive as well as defensive ego functions; and
(c) The patient and the analyst have to set therapeutic and life goals consonant with the patient's temperamental traits and functional abilities.

CHAPTER NINE

Counselling Parents and Early Intervention

The importance of informed, supportive counselling for the parents of children with developmental deviations cannot be overestimated. We emphasize the term "informed" because counselling is most effective when it is founded upon a solid understanding of the deviation and its effects. Counselling parents is an essential component of any early intervention aimed at relief or prevention of emotional difficulties generated by developmental causes; in many cases it is the *only* intervention needed. The following case illustrates such early intervention:[*]

> Laura was 28 months old when her parents requested consultation because of excessive crying, "crankiness" and poor frustration tolerance. The parents were young graduate students, highly intelligent, warm and emotionally very invested in caring for Laura, their only child. Her early developmental history had been unremarkable except for excessive neonatal jaundice and delayed walking (15 months). In fact her cognitive development was precocious: she had a vocabulary of twenty to thirty words by the age of twelve months, and she had taught herself to read a few words from TV commercials (e.g., "Toys R Us") by the age of two. Her parents took great pride in her precociousness and encouraged her.
>
> The examination revealed that Laura was, indeed intellectually precocious, but significantly delayed in motor development. She was slightly hypotonic, her gross movements were clumsy, appropriate for fifteen-month level. Laura's walking was wobbly, she could not climb and descend stairs freely, nor could she jump. Laura seemed aware of her difficulties and very sensitive to failure. She cried easily when encountering difficulties, refused to try some of the tasks or demanded help.
>
> The parents were given an explanation of the problem, adivsed to emphasize less the child's intellectual achievements and to engage in a

[*] Reprinted from the Journal of the American Academy of Child and Adolescent Psychiatry, 1987,26/4:583, by kind permission of the American Academy of Child and Adolescent Psychiatry.

systematic progressive training of motor skills, by means of suitable games. The results were gratifying. Laura's motor skills improved considerably within two months and so did her mood. She became more relaxed, less prone to crying and showed better frustration tolerance. She took delight in the various jumping and climbing games her parents invented for her and dared to try tasks she had shunned previously.

The type of counselling and its objectives will be dictated by the needs of each family but the overall approach is based on six principles:

(a) Making a thorough diagnostic assessment of the child's impairments *and abilities,* and sharing it with the parents and the child;
(b) Helping the parents to devise child-rearing methods suitable for their child's idosyncratic needs;
(c) Improving impaired or delayed functions by practice or other means;
(d) Helping the child to use "detours" to compensate for functional deficits;
(e) Promoting and encouraging well-developed functions;
(f) Accepting the child and his developmental idiosyncrasy.

(a) A thorough assessment of a child's motor, perceptual, cognitive and emotional development is essential. It is the foundation of any rational intervention plan, but it also serves other functions. The diagnosis is essential in order to establish a therapeutic alliance with the child and the parents, to dispel fears and fantasies and to instill in them a trust in the professional who is well-informed and familiar with the bewildering array of problems they are facing. We have discussed the discouragement and helplessness caused by the breakdown of empathic dialogue, i.e., reciprocal reinforcement, between the infant and the caregiver. The parents' frustration and confusion are compounded by criticism and conflicting advice offered by well-intentioned but misguided relatives, friends and professionals who are not fully aware of the nature of the problem. It is an immense relief to encounter someone who offers not merely support but conceptual grasp and emotional understanding of their plight. Presenting the family with the broad outlines of a plan for action is equally reassuring. In the milder cases, like that of Laura, helping the parents to understand the problem and suggesting basic guidelines may be all that is needed. Many parents that we have counselled were able to mobilize enough psychological resources of their own to help the child. One cannot fail to be impressed by the courage, wisdom and perseverance some of those parents display. Yet love and determination are seldom enough; most parents need at least enlightenment as to the nature of the problem and guidelines for coping, based on a developmental assessment.

Many parents have unspoken questions that need to be explored. "Am I a bad parent? Have I damaged my child, physically or emotionally? Is it hereditary? Is my child retarded; is he going to be insane?" The best reassurance is to bring such fantasies to the surface and to answer questions openly. It often helps to share the diagnostic criteria with the parents. For instance, the profile of an intelligence test can be used to demonstrate graphically the gap between potential and "average" performance and the meaning of functional impairments: "This is how bright your child is at his best and this is where he fails."

We explain to the parents that occasional concrete cognition or a lapse in assessing social reality are common symptoms of neuropsychological impairment and not a sign of insanity. We explain that a child who is able to maintain object relationships, e.g. an affectionate relationship with a school friend, is certainly not suffering from childhood schizophrenia. One of the important issues to clarify is the child's low self-esteem. Parents need to understand that some of the disturbing things that those children say or do are clumsy attempts to protect their vulnerable narcissism or to compensate, by means of childish self-aggrandizement, for feelings of incompetence and worthlessness. Above all, parents need to know that the *child's low self-esteem is an inevitable result of developmental deviation and not in itself a proof of poor parenting.* Last, not least, sharing the diagnostic process with the parents allows us to present an intervention plan that makes sense to them to secure their participation. In presenting the intervention plan we emphasize that patience and perseverance do produce results, no matter how painful the situation may be at present. At the same time we caution the parents that some of the objectives take a long time, perhaps years, to achieve, and that new developmental stages, such as entering school or adolescence, may well bring with them new problems to cope with. Cognitive and emotional development in such children seems often not only delayed but uneven; it seems to proceed at spurts that are difficult to predict. A child, who has been emotionally immature, clinging and absorbed in wish-fulfilling fantasy, will suddenly mature, assume new responsibilities and join his peers in age-adequate activities. Cognitive abilities also mature late and by leaps. Behavior may mature, but it may also regress, especially during adolescence.

Diagnostic assessment, though essential, is not free of potential side effects. Labelling the child as "different", "deviant" or "impaired" may lead to self-fulfilling expectation of failure or maladjustment. This is especially true if schools or other community agencies are involved prematurely. A label of "normalcy" may be more helpful in some cases than any special treatment by community agencies, and parents who resist involving the community may be right.

(b) We have already described how children's developmental idiosyncrasies induce the parents to adopt unusual and often counter-productive child-rearing practices. The task of the clinician is to help the parents to devise handling methods that will be reasonably effective without interfering with long-range developmental objectives. The following example will illustrate such a simple yet effective intervention.

Amos was a slightly pre-term boy born after several miscarriages. A breach presentation required general anaesthesia, but there was no significant fetal distress. He was healthy, with slight signs of immaturity, such as frequent tremors. His parents requested consultation when he was ten days old. They were concerned because Amos was difficult to handle: he responed negatively to many visual and auditory stimuli, cried a great deal and resisted changing diapers, washing or other physical contact. He could not be soothed by hugging and displayed the characteristics of a "non-cuddly" baby (Brazelton, 1973). In view of the child's apparent over-sensitivity we suggested reducing the amount of tactile stimuli, keeping the baby well wrapped, cuddled-up in a small cradle, and avoiding excessive light or noise. He seemed to be perfectly happy in that low-stimulus, as-if-intrauterine condition. We noticed that Amos, when awake, was most comfortable in a situation of limited body contact, freedom of movement and a wide visual field. We encouraged the parents to accomodate themselves to the child's preferences. Mother did so by holding the baby leaning on her lap and father by carrying him propped against the shoulder. The tension was reduced and the interaction became much more enjoyable. Eventually, a gradual and progressive exposure to more stimuli enabled the boy and his parents to engage in a normal and rich "mediated learning" experience and to develop a close emotional relationship. In this case a simple but timely intervention averted a potentially serious difficulty in parent-child relationship.

The special needs of the "difficult" child require patience and flexibility, because they change as the child develops. In infants, soothing techniques and monitoring of stimulation are usually the crucial issues. Later on, children with developmental deviations may need more guidance in organizing their time, e.g. eating and sleeping patterns, and play and work activities. Children whose impulse control is impaired need more supervision and a firm, consistent structure.

The guiding principle for taking care of a child with developmental deviation can be defined in the following way: *Whenever a regulatory ego function is delayed or impaired, the parents have to substitute for it an external auxiliary ego.* Such a need for external ego support, however, should not hinder the child's emotional growth and in particular his autonomy and sense of responsibility. This requires flexibility; one has to be willing to proceed by trial and error if need be. The parents also have to confront the child's inappropriate behaviors while avoiding further narcissistic injury and damage to his self-esteem. They have to learn how to supervise closely without being intrusive. All that is, indeed, a formidable task that may take a long time to master.

(c) Once a developmental lag has been diagnosed the parents will wish to know whether and how it can be corrected. Many techniques have been described and are being practiced by speech therapists, physiotherapists, occupational therapists, and other auxilliary professions. There is considerable controversy whether a functional deficit due, presumably, to innate maturational causes can be improved by environmental manipulation and how much. In our experience many functions can be improved to some extent by exercise, practice and a system of awards. Even in those cases in which the direct effect of treatment on functional maturation is slight, a systematic program of activities counteracts the feelings of helpessness and the tendency to avoidance, which often do more harm than the primary impairment itself. The type of activity and its amount depend on the individual needs; the decision of who should implement the treatment program is also important. Many activities can be conducted by the parents provided they receive an initial instruction; what they lack in professional skills is compensated for by the emotional relationship with the child, which is a critical factor in motivating children, especially the younger ones. In other cases, especially in older children, the opposite may be true: an outsider, e.g. a tutor, may be in a better position than a parent to make demands. Delegating the task and the responsibility for progress to an outsider helps to eliminate areas of friction in the family. For some parents, laboring under pressure of guilt and worry, the additional burden of responsibility is simply too much, while others find relief in the opportunity to "do something".

Some functions, e.g. attention or impulse control, can be improved by medication. In such cases, too, the informed participation of the parents is crucial in order to set up and maintain a rational program of pharmacotherapy.

(d) "Detours" are alternative methods for accomplishing a task in spite of an impaired funciton, e.g. a color-blind person may rely on the fact that the red traffic light is always above the green one. Parents need to understand that what appears to be a strange behavior or an unreasonable demand on part of the child may be a groping attempt to bypass a disability, i.e. to find a "detour". Some "detours" consist of a device, e.g. a typewriter for a child whose hand-writing is unintelligible, others depend on substituting one function for another, e.g. using visual instead of auditory memory, as Mr. Y. did (Chapter Three). Some subjects invent highly ingenious methods, like the boy with a partial nominal aphasia, i.e. occasional inability to recall words (Chapter Five), who memorized sentences from textbooks and used them to construct compositions. Not all children are imaginative enough to invent "detours" and it becomes the task of the parents and the therapist to suggest and encourage any effective method for reducing disability.

(e) The main goal of promoting *well-developed abilities* is to enhance self-esteem. A child who is expected to persist patiently in tasks, which for him are difficult and frustrating, needs also to excel in some other activities to boost his morale. The impact of accomplishment is illustrated by the following case:

> Mr. K. had a fairly typical history of an undiagnosed learning-disabled child. In spite of very good intelligence he had acquired only elementary academic skills and dropped out of high school. He was an embittered, suspicious, unsociable man, alienated from his original family, in conflict with his wife and distant from his children. His only consolation was hard physical work and soccer, which he played with relish. He rejected any suggestion of treatment or counselling and even refused to meet with the school psychologist who was treating one of his sons. He never read books and could not help his children with their school work because he did not understand it.
>
> Somehow Mr. K. discovered the hobby of making silver jewelry. He became engrossed in that hobby and developed it into a part-time business. Mr. K. demonstrated considerable creative talent and dexterity in this highly competitive occupation. It would be exaggerating to claim that Mr. K.'s basic personality changed completely. Yet there was an amazing change in his life: he enjoyed his new work and shared it with the family, became much more self-confident and less quarrelsome. The most impressive change occurred in the relationship with his children: he enjoyed their company and found common interests to share. Surprisingly, a creative outlet succeeded where the psychotherapist's efforts failed.

For some children, engaging in an activity that provides opportunities for developing competences, as well as for sublimation of drives, can do more to foster emotional growth than psychotherapy. Accomplishments not only promote sense of competence and counteract the injury to self-esteem, but also enhance the social standing of the child who had been rejected or ignored by his peers.

The parents of a child with developmental deviations need, however, to assume a balancing role. On the one hand they support the child's quest for areas of competence. On the other hand they should not collude with his attempts to use such activities as a cover-up or excuse for not confronting his difficulties.

(f) The final task that the parents of a child with developmental deviations face is in some cases the most difficult one. It is to accept the child and his idiosyncrasies, to re-evaluate their image of him, and to help the child to rehabilitate his self-image. The therapist who assists the parents in this task works

primarily in the framework of psychoanalytic theory of intrapsychic dynamics and interpersonal relationships. Revaluating
the child's image in the eyes of his parents and exploring his
role in the family involves working through the parent's feelings of disappointment, narcissistic hurt, anger and guilt. It
may also involve an exploration of the parents' unresolved
conflicts and neurotic needs.

The following case, which has been mentioned previously
(Chapter Four), illustrates the meshing-in of a child's impairment with a parent's unresolved emotional conflict:

Mr. G. was a young patient with a history of mild cerebral palsy whose
major symptoms included a paralyzing fear of his own aggression. As a
child he had been prone to violent rages, which evoked harsh verbal
attacks from his father. Mr. G.'s father was a highly successful and
vigorous attorney, who had considerable difficulties in expressing or
sublimating his aggression outside the courtroom. He was a convinced
liberal and detested the militant patriotism and idolation of the military
prevalent at that time. He was reluctant to assert himself at home or
among friends (except when drinking) but was quite capable of becoming enraged and abusive when aroused. During Mr. G.'s therapy it
became clear how the father's inability to deal with his own aggression
compounded the patient's problems of impaired impulse control. The
impulsive angry boy became the father's externalized evil self and that
image of "little Hitler" became incorporated into Mr. G.'s own negative,
hated self. This process was illustrated by a fantasy recounted by the
patient: "A great hunter in Africa suffers from spells of a mysterious
illness during which he retires to his tent. It transpires that during bouts
of the illness his body becomes covered with boils which burst, releasing
little horrible-looking black devils, an embodiment of sheer evil."

This fantasy expressed two preconscious ideas: (a) Mr. G's
wish to get rid of the evil, hateful part of his self, in a manner
consistent with the patient's paranoid personality traits, i.e. by
projection, and (b) Mr. G's perception of his relationship with
the father. The "great white hunter", i.e. the father, gives birth
to a horrible little creature to purge himself of evil, that is to
recover from "illness".

This case illustrates how the reconstruction of the genesis of
a symptom or character trait reveals a convergence between the
parent's unresolved emotional conflicts and the child's innate
impairment; in this case failure of impulse control. This point
will be elaborated further in the chapter on reconstruction.

Here we wish merely to illustrate how counselling parents may require exploration of and insight to those emotional conflicts that have a bearing on their perception of the child.

In conclusion, counselling parents of a child with developmental deviation is based on an assessment of the child's developmental impairments and idiosyncrasies as well as an understanding of the emotional dynamics of the family. In order to reduce the negative effects of a deviation on the shaping of a child's personality, we need to understand the emotional impact of the developmental deviation on the child and on his environment. At the same time we need insight into those unresolved emotional conflicts of the parents that enmesh with the child's difficulties. We also need to recognize and to foster the psychological resources and the motivation of the parents, as well as the personality assets of the child. Various therapeutic modalities improve the child's functional ability and enhance his competence. Confronting the basic emotional issues of the child and of his parents requires, however, a psychoanalytic frame of reference, even though the actual therapeutic technique may vary according to the individual circumstances of each case.

CHAPTER TEN

Psychoanalytic Reconstruction and Developmental Individuality

Reconstruction is an area of psychoanalysis and dynamic psychotherapy for which developmental theory is particularly relevant. Psychoanalysis introduced reconstruction of childhood experiences and shaped it into a therapeutic tool of primary importance. Other modalities, such as analysis of transference and analysis of defences, were subsequently devised, but reconstruction remains one of the mainstays of analytic therapy and theory (Blum, 1980). All methods of dynamic psychotherapy incorporate some measure of inquiry into childhood experiences and their relevance to a patient's present difficulties. The task of reconstruction is not merely to uncover repressed infantile wishes and traumatic events of childhood, but also to integrate them with the adult personality: a man's or woman's loves and hates, his or her values, fears and hopes.

Reconstruction in analysis is not a mere intellectual exercise. In order for it to be therapeutically effective, the affect of the childhood event has to be re-experienced by the patient. The analyst guides the patient using his own feelings as cues. Sometimes he identifies with the patient as a child, sometimes with the parent, if the patient casts him in that role, sometimes with both. In other words, analysis of transference and analysis of counter-transference open the way for reconstruction, while recollection of childhood events and fantasies provides validation of analysis of transference. This synergistic exploration of transference and reconstruction constitutes the fabric of psychoanalysis.

We cannot fully understand the events of a patient's childhood unless we study them in the context of his development, i.e., the developmental stage in which they occurred, and his developmental individuality, be it a temperamental idiosyncracy or impairment. In the previous chapters, we have examined the effects of deviations on development; in this chapter we illustrate a clinical approach that integrates developmental insight into therapeutic reconstruction.

> Mrs. C., whose case has been mentioned previously (Ch.IV), was a divorced woman in her early thirties, a highly capable research scientist, who came to treatment because of a sense of pervasive unhappiness and dissatisfaction with her lifestyle: "I live next to life", in her words. Her work was humdrum, her mood was mostly depressed and her love relationships invariably led to heartbreak. She felt inhibited, at times overcome by anxiety and had a very low opinion of herself.
>
> As a child she had been very attached to her intellectual, aloof, biologist father, whom she admired greatly. Mrs. C. had always resented her mother, and described her as controlling, overcritical and insensitive to Mrs. C.'s emotional needs. The mother objected to Mrs. C.'s boyfriends, clothes, and recreations; she had been particularly vigorous in her criticism of Mrs. C.'s passivity, lack of initiative and preference for lying down and leisurely enjoying reading or listening to music.
>
> Passivity, over-compliance and lack of initiative were also prominent in the patient's adult life and in analysis.

The analyst became aware of conflicting feelings; an empathic identification with the forlorn, lonely girl, and an increasing impatience with the slow progress of treatment. This attitude of impatience and a wish to "push" the patient were so similar to the description of Mrs. C.'s mother that they were interpreted as a projective identification with the unempathic, pushing mother. The analyst shared with the patient the feeling that she was casting him in her mother's role. Mrs. C. seemed encouraged by the interpretation and seemingly relieved at not being attacked or criticized; yet the slow, plodding treatment went on. The analyst, therefore, felt that something was amiss in the dynamic assessment.

Two points that emerged from the clinical data seemed in need of further clarification:

(a) In spite of Mrs. C.'s strong indictment of her mother's attitudes and bitter arguments between the two, one could feel an undercurrent of genuine caring by daughter and mother alike. Indeed, Mrs. C.'s mother emerged from the description as an intrusive, over-critical mother, but not an uncaring or cold person at all.

(b) The patient's passivity was not just an expression of negativism. Somewhat timidly she described her moments of serene enjoyment: reading a book by the lakeshore or listening to a concert. The analyst interpreted this as a plea to understand that her passive pleasures were not always idle or contrary and the interpretation was received with relief. Mrs. C. agreed that some of her best moments were passive and leisurely, but she herself took the initiative to point out that her passivity served also as a form of timid defiance toward the mother.

We could now reassess the dynamics of Mrs. C.'s childhood. She had been a slow child, with poor gross motor coordination (she still lacked the sense of balance), inattentive and timid. Her spatial orientation was poor and she relied on visual clues to find her way: in darkness or in a fog she would panic. We have often observed that poor motor development undermines a child's sense of competence and his self-esteem, and fosters a passive-dependent relationship with the mother. Moreover, an impairment of spatial orientation seems to delay autonomy and foster separation anxiety (Chapter Six). It was not difficult now to understand the nature of the early relationship. Mrs. C.'s mother was a vivacious, emotional, restless woman, warm but impatient and quick-tempered. She was also a competent, vigorous and competitive business woman. Such a person could never understand nor cope with a slow, clumsy, clinging child, without becoming exasperated and critical. The message conveyed to the little girl was not "I don't want you", but "I want you close to me but can't you ever do something right?" The situation was made worse by mother's unhappiness with her marriage and father's failure to provide emotional support for the girl, even though he was very attached to her. Having despaired of ever living up to her mother's standards and expectations, the little girl found a measure of comfort in negativism, which allowed her to exert some control and give vent to her suppressed rage. The price for it was an internalization of an extremely negative, over-critical view of herself. This, in turn, combined with guilt over unresolved Oedipal ambivalence, contributed to the development of a self-defeating, masochistic life-style.

We will not attempt to present here all the complexities of

this patient's unconscious conflicts as they emerged in a lengthy analysis. The point we want to make is that at that particular stage of treatment an empathic understanding of Mrs. C.'s temperamental individuality, combined with an understanding of her mother's reaction to it, facilitated and enriched a therapeutically effective reconstruction. This was shown in several ways:

(a) There was a dramatic change in Mrs. C.'s relationship with her mother, which became more relaxed and more mature;
(b) There was a perceptible strengthening of the therapeutic alliance;
(c) The reconstruction was followed by recollection of considerable amount of childhood memories and aspects of relationships with both parents, of which the patient had not been aware previously;
(d) Insight into the "misfit" between the patient's and her mother's temperament led to exploration of Mrs. C.'s difficulties in her feminine identification and to a reevaluation of her ego ideals. She no longer felt compelled to achieve mother's efficiency or social adroitness, began to explore her natural inclinations and to shape them into adaptive patterns.

In summary, the developmental understanding did not replace, but complemented and facilitated the psychoanalytic process of interpretation of transference, exploration of defences and resolution of unconscious conflicts, strengthening of true self and reassessment of ego-ideals.

Another example is provided by Mr. Y., whose case has been mentioned in Chapter Three. Mr. Y. presented himself as "a worker in his father's tool factory"; in reality he was a well-trained and gifted mechanical engineer. Mr. Y.'s life was a chain of underachievement, submissiveness and self-defeating behavior, including the marriage to a severely disturbed, aggressive woman.

Mr. Y. was eager to be helped, but progress in therapy was slow. There seemed to be little continuity between the sessions; clarifications and interpretations were forgotten. Analysis of the failure to remember the content of sessions led to the discovery of a specific impairment of sequential auditory memory (Chapter Three). The therapist's initial interpretation, i.e., that forgetting her comments had been an expression of negativism, was not entirely mistaken, but had to be revised. Mr. Y. was indeed affected by an innate impairment which became inextricably ingrained into his emotional development and object relationships. When he was motivated, e.g., during his college studies, he struggled to overcome the impairment by coping devices, e.g., the use of visual memory. When he felt frustrated or threatened his poor memory became a tool of passive aggression and negativism.

We could now formulate a hypothesis regarding Mr. Y.'s childhood. His family had been conflict-ridden and unhappy, and his mother, a deeply frustrated woman, was seductive and intensely angry at the same time. The three children assumed their respective roles: the older brother rebelled against the mother and left home at an early age, the younger sister became a "model", compliant child, and Mr. Y. became the "dumb" one, strongly attached to his mother and the target of her verbal and physical aggression. This role was assigned to him in a large measure because he was perceived as "uncooperative" and unreliable: forgetting instructions, repeating mistakes, or failing to change undesirable habits.

When Mr. Y. entered school his neuropsychological impairment resulted in academic underachievement. The learning disability was never recognized, perhaps because his very high intelligence allowed him to cope with the school's demands, but his mediocre performance reinforced greatly his negative self-image of a "dunce" and his role as the scapegoat of the family.

We could now see the link between Mr. Y.'s childhood experiences and his submissive, masochistic relationship toward women and his need to cast them into the role of a seductive ogress, desirable and threatening alike. That need motivated his disastrous marriage and it was also expressed in transference fantasies. His intense, but inhibited aggression was either directed against himself or found an outlet in anal stubbornness and neglect of personal hygiene. His self-inflicted failures, in school, at home and in therapy were both an expression of self-hatred and a way to take revenge against the objects of his love-hate: "I am a dunce, an incompetent, bungling fool, but you, my mother, my wife, my therapist, are just as stupid and incompetent as I am." That particular dynamic constellation was the convergence of two factors: family dynamics and Mr. Y.'s innate impairments. The latter determined the choice of Mr. Y. as the favorite target for his mother's seething rage; they also led Mr. Y. to develop the self-image of an incompetent fool and to use failures as a means of revenge.

In conclusion, psychoanalytic reconstruction may be facilitated and enriched by insight into the patient's temperamental idiosyncrasies and developmental lags and impairments. Understanding a child's temperament and developmental pattern adds a significant dimension and brings alive his yearnings, fantasies and pain. Moreover, it helps the patient and the analyst to get a more complete picture of the parents' behavior and motivations, and to introduce an element of objective reassessment of childhood events. Reconstruction, as we said before, is not merely an emotional catharsis. It is also an integration of childhood experiences with the patient's adult personality. An ability to reassess objectively the parents' past behavior paves the way for resolving infantile idealizations or vilifications of the parent, which are often the last residue of infantile fantasies of parental omnipotence. Unconscious fantasies of parental omnipotence are hard to dispel. Some apparently successfully completed analyses have not, it seems, confronted the problem adequately. Therapists are tempted to accept too readily their patients' subjective perception of the parents, and shades of parental omnipotence find their way even into some theoretical analytical formulations.

The sobering realization that adequate caregiving is a complex interaction between baby, parent and environment helps to take a more balanced view of a patient's personal past as well as of psychoanalytic theory of development.

CHAPTER ELEVEN

Cognition and Psychoanalysis

Clinical observation of subjects with developmental deviations, as well as experimental investigations of human development, require a revision of some conventional psychoanalytic postulates. Certain formulations have to be modified; others appear valid but need to be incorporated into a broader context. It is no longer possible to study the development of psychic structures and of emotional relationships separately from the development of other functions. This chapter deals with the links between cognitive and emotional processes during child development and in psychoanalysis. In the next chapter, we will outline a comprehensive model of child development.

A. Cognition, affects and object-relationships

The role of perception and of cognition in the development of psychic structures is taken for granted by psychoanalytic investigators, but rarely studied in any detail. For instance, it is self-evident that an infant cannot develop attachment to his caregiver unless he can perceive and recognize her. It is assumed, therefore, that the infant learns to recognize those subjects who provide him with basic comforts and need gratification, such as feeding. Repeated gratifying or frustrating experiences coalesce gradually into good and bad object- and self-representations (Kernberg, 1980, 1984). In other words, the basic postulate of psychoanalytic theory of development is that the infant learns to recognize his mother because she provides pleasure and comfort. Liss (1955) outline in detail the "classic" psychoanalytic view of learning. His discussion is based on drive-discharge theory and learning is seen basically as sublimation of drives. The relationship with the teacher is a continuation of parent-child relationships; therefore the teacher as parent substitute motivates the child to learn. We may sum up that point of view in two postulates:

(a) The infant loves his mother, or caregiver, because she satisfies his needs, and therefore he learns from her;
(b) The child learns from his teacher because she is a parent-substitute, i.e., he loves her.

This rather simplistic formulation is correct as far as it goes, but it fails to account for the complex relationship between cognitive and emotional processes. Investigators of cognitive development (Piaget, 1952) and investigators of affective development (Sroufe, 1979) emphasize that affects are indispensable components of any cognitive process. Affects express the subjective significance of cognition, enhance the effectiveness of cognitive process, stimulate learning and assure the integration of cognition with all the other psychological processes. Cognitive processes also *generate* affects. It is generally recognized, for instance, that a successful cognitive operation produces a sense of well-being because it evokes self-satisfaction. Investigators of infant behavior, however, have demonstrated that the connection between effective cognition and positive affect is much more basic than self-satisfaction; indeed, it goes back to a stage when neither self-satisfaction nor self-awareness even exist. H. Papoušek and his team (Papoušek & Papoušek, 1983; Koester et al., 1987) have been able to demonstrate that in infants barely a few months old a successful cognitive operation, such as recognition of a familiar percept or perception of an *expected* stimulus, evokes positive affect. The reverse happens when a cognitive operation fails: the infant shows signs of perplexity and distress. Later on, the infant learns to *initiate* expected events by a process of operant or instrumental conditioning, such as moving a mobile by kicking it, or making a sound by shaking a rattle. Infants also learn to engage the caregivers in "games" of reciprocal smiling or vocalizations; in other words, social operant conditioning.

Infants delight in those little games, while older children spend endless hours listening to a favorite story, told in exactly the same manner. It is the *familiarity* and the *expectability* that make those events gratifying.

Freud was puzzled by the deep-rooted need to relive familiar experiences and it led him to speculate on repetition-compulsion (Freud, 1920). Before embarking on the quasi-philosophical issue of biological entropy (i.e., the need to return to a previous state), Freud observed that repetition in children is pleasurable because it enhances a sense of mastery, replacing a passively endured past experience by a deliberate, active deed. Unfortunately, Freud never elaborated on this line of thought any further and never attempted to reconcile the pleasure of mastery with his theory of pleasure as discharge of drives and reduction of tension. The pleasure of mastery received considerable attention from other investigators (Hunt, 1965). R.W. White, after an extensive review of evidence, concluded that the sense of mastery, which he called "effectance", should be considered a drive, an "intrinsic motivation" in its own right (White, 1959). It seems to us, however, that the need for competence can best be conceived of as a manifestation of narcissism. Narcissism is self-love; in this instance, it is invested on one's own cognition, perception, motility, and other ego functions, all of which are components of self-representation.

An ineffectual exercise of an ego function is experienced as unpleasurable, whereas a successful operation of a motor, perceptual or cognitive function is perceived as pleasurable. A repetition of such pleasurable experiences leads to a sense of competence and to an enhanced, healthy narcissism, i.e., increased self-regard (see Chapter Four).

The pleasure inherent in a successful operation of ego functions calls for a review of the "economic" principle of mental functioning. The economic principle was succinctly defined by Freud as the need "to free the mental apparatus entirely from excitation or to keep the amount of excitation constant or to keep it as low as possible" (Freud, 1920, p. 62). Hence, drive discharge and reduction of excitation are pleasurable. Freud was aware that not all pleasurable experiences can be easily construed as release of tension and the relationship between pleasure and drive discharge has been the subject of discussion in psychoanalytical literature since then. A developmental approach will help us to redefine the economic principle of mental functioning. It is true that a baby in distress is comforted by release of tension; nevertheless, "keeping the mental apparatus at a constant or lowest possible level of excitation" is the last thing that can be said of a developing organism. A child of any age, even an infant, initiates a host of activities aimed exclusively at self-stimulation, at *increasing* the level of excitation. Children love stimulating play and even infants find ways to entice the caregivers to engage in exciting games. Moreover, children enjoy novel stimuli provided the experience is not too overwhelming or confusing. Children also engage in tasks not only in order to overcome a problem, but seemingly for the sake of consolidating the cognitive process which was required for that task (Karmiloff-Smith, 1986).

L. Koester et al. (1987) have suggested that pleasurable affect is not related to the *level* of tension, but to the *degree of integration* of mental processes. They apply H. Werner's model, which conceives of development as progressive differentiation and organization (Werner, 1961; Werner & Kaplan, 1963). Stechler (1982) calls a living organism a "self-organizing system". We may say that human beings, and perhaps all living organisms, have an intrinsic need to maintain a continuous process of successive differentiation and integration. Human beings of all ages, but children in particular, search vigorously for stimuli that induce further differentiation of mental operations and then strive to integrate the new process into preexisting configurations.

We can reformulate the economic principle of mental functioning as follows: *An increase of integration of the mental apparatus is experienced as pleasurable.* Freud's original formulation is incorporated in this expanded one, because relief from tension is pleasurable, insofar as it facilitates reintegration.

An excessively intense stimulation, whether intrinsic, e.g., sexual arousal, or extrinsic, e.g., a "traumatic event", cannot be integrated and generates distress. Only a release of tension will enable the organism to integrate the experience. Our new way of defining the economic principle explains why such diverse situations as mastering a cognitive task, absorbing a novel stimulus *or* release of drive, can be equally pleasurable.

Having examined the relationship between ego functions and pleasure we can return to the topic of early object relationships. We realize now that a mother is a source of positive affect not only because she comforts the baby and provides him with drive-satisfaction, but also because she provides him with a host of pleasurable *cognitive* experiences. Her face, her voice, her movements, the touch and smell of her body, soon become familiar and hence an unending stream of recognition experiences. We need to reformulate the psychoanalytic view of attachment in the following way: The baby recognizes his mother because he enjoys her closeness; *he also enjoys her closeness because he keeps recognizing her over and over again.*

Later on, the mother and other caregivers participate actively in a child's growing mastery of his body, his environment and his mind. Although the child explores his body and his environment on his own initiative, the caregivers provide him with "mediated learning" (Feuerstein, 1979). The caregiver provides stimulating objects, e.g., offers toys or lifts a baby to the switch to turn on the lights. She (or he) models motor acts, e.g., how to put a block in a jar, or shapes them by moving a baby's hand. She associates percepts with words and interprets to the infant his own states of mind, e.g., "You got scared, Johnny, right?", or "Johnny wants to play with Mummy's keys?" Such mediated teaching, which is normally done intuitively, with the caregiver being barely aware of it, is a crucial stimulus for early learning, but also an intensely affective experience. The pleasure derived from successful mediated learning is a powerful factor in cementing the early object relationship. We need to differentiate, in that context, between early infancy and the latter part of the first year. During early infancy feeding is a unique emotional experience. As the infant develops, however, and his interaction with the caregiver becomes more complex, other forms of need gratification and mediated learning become more important. Rutter (1977), after reviewing studies of attachment, concluded that feeding is *not* the critical factor in the formation of attachment. The most important factors are *playing* with the child, especially if the caregiver is sensitive to the child's signals, and *comforting* the infant in distress. Playing effectively implies being attuned to the infant's ability to cope with the stimulus or the task presented. In other words, the caregiver facilitates states of enhanced integration, either by relief from excessive tension or by mediated teaching. The caregiver who facilitates integration becomes the object of attachment.

Such as expanded model of infant-caregiver relationship helps us to understand better the early and intense attachment of many infants to their fathers and to clarify the role of the father in early child development.

The role of the father in early development is receiving increasing attention (Lamb, 1981). It has been recognized that the father-infant relationship facilitates a successful resolution of the symbiotic bond (Mahler and Gosliner, 1955). In Western societies the role of the father in the family has changed conspicuously, reflecting a tendency towards a more egalitarian model of family. There is a more equal distribution of both child-rearing and economic responsibilities, and bottle-feeding has removed the last constraint on sharing baby care between husband and wife. Many young fathers of today participate enthusiastically in the burden and the joy of the physical care of their babies.

We find, however, many fathers who participate only marginally in the physical care of their infants and yet become objects of intense attachment. That is explained by the fact that those fathers take an active interest in their babies and *play* with them. The expanded economic model explains how the pleasure inherent in the practice of ego functions makes the "mediating" parent an object of attachment not less intense than the attachment to caregivers who provide biological needs and comforts. Later on, as the child enters school, it is the teacher who assumes the main responsibility for the child's cognitive growth. She, or he, becomes a parent-substitute, a mediator between the child and his expanding world. In such manner, the teacher becomes a provider of pleasurable experiences which accompany the progress of cognitive integration (assuming that the teacher accomplishes her task as she should). The second postulate of psycho-analytical theory of learning should be reformulated in the following way: "A child learns from his teacher because he loves her, *but he also loves the teacher because he learns from her.*

B. Cognitive factors in transference and in therapeutic alliance: The learning process in psychoanalysis

Transference is such a ubiquitous and inevitable phenomenon that we hardly stop to ask ourselves what is the moving force behind it. It is assumed that the patient's need of and hope for relief from suffering create a situation of emotional dependence which, in turn, mobilizes infantile needs and fantasies. This formulation, though plausible enough, does not seem to be the complete answer. The emotional dependence is often so intense that it appears to be an effect of transference rather than a reason for it. The hoped-for relief is very real, but often located in a distant future, far too remote to quell an infantile need for immediate comfort. The libidinal strivings activated by regression are hardly gratified. The patient's realistic, adult, assessment of the help he is receiving and trust in the therapist's ability and dedication, i.e., the therapeutic alliance, is a sustaining force in the painful and frustrating process, but is it all?

Our analysis of cognitive factors in object relationship relationships allows us to discern an additional force that enhances transference and, at the same time, sustains the process of analysis and shapes it. That force is the emotional impact of learning. The central aim of analysis is acquisition of insight, and insight is, above all, an integrative learning experience. It combines in a harmonious manner emotions, reasoning, remote and recent memories, and sometimes also a creative element in the form of metaphor (Aleksandrowicz, 1962). The sudden enlightenment which sometimes happens during analysis (the so-called "A-ha" experience) is not only therapeutically effective but also intensely gratifying; the more common, slow and gradual development of inslight, however, is also gratifying and sustains motivation. The satisfaction of insight is not limited to the intellectual, who is used to searching for knowledge and for whom self-understanding may well be a conscious motive for requesting analysis. Unsophisticated, but intellectually alert people, who request treatment solely for the relief of distress and have no inkling of what awareness of one's deeper self means, can easily become motivated to embark on self-exploration and find the process satisfying.

The positive affect generated by understanding and enhanced self-awareness not only sustains motivation, but also helps the patient to contain distress and to cope with anxiety. This is illustrated by the following example:

At a late state of Mrs. J's analysis we were finally able to confront her fears of social contact. This had been a very difficult subject for her, associated with fears of insanity or a fantasy of having a brain disease. It transpired that any friendly conversation would, sooner or later, lead to a mounting anxiety which forced the patient to withdraw, in panic, either by becoming detached and inattentive or by terminating the encounter. If the patient felt sexual attraction or suppressed envy the situation would be worse, but even in the absence of any threatening instinctual wish, in a neutral situation, the anxiety did arise inevitably. We were finally able to understand that the anxiety was an expression of fear of fusion, of becoming absorbed, in a literal sense, into the other's personality. Being intensely attentive to another person's thoughts and feelings (otherwise Mrs. J. would soon lose the trend of the conversation) resulted, after some length of time, in a strange feeling of inner emptiness, leading to a transient loss of sense of self, as if she no longer had an existence of her own. This borderline-like experience may have been facilitated by Mrs. J.'s attention deficit; in any case, it was extremely frightening. It reminded her of having once experienced a strange sensation as if she had no skin and the world around her was penetrating into her body.

Mrs. J. observed that such experiences of loss of self did not happen when she was angry; in her words: "When I am angry I am stronger". At this point the analyst explained to the patient how a toddler uses aggression and oppositional behavior (which was also a prominent feature of Mrs. J.'s personality) to facilitate separation and individuation. He explained that an absence of oppositional behavior at that age is not a sign of healthy development. Mrs. J. said: "From what I have been told I must have been a very compliant child, hardly oppositional at all".

The remarkable feature of that session was that in spite of an inner turmoil, and in spite of the patient's great sensitivity in regard to the issues discussed, she remained relatively composed. Her comments had a serene undertone and towards the end of the session she said: "You may think that I am peculiar, but I feel as if I were standing outside and examining myself; actually it is quite interesting."

This session illustrates how organizing one's experiences and gaining insight enhance a sense of mastery and help the patient to confront highly distressful subjects with relative equanimity.

Organizing one's internal world, i.e., acquisition of insight, is a learning process but it is not the only learning experience in therapy. A patient learns also to behave differently, to consider courses of action which had been unthinkable before. That happens because some neurotic behavior patterns are due to simple inhibition, i.e., wanting but not daring, while other behavioral symptoms cover repression, i.e., inability to even *consider* an act that could reveal warded-off wishes.

The following is an example of repression that prevented a patient from considering action alternatives:

> Mrs. Q., whose case has been mentioned in Ch. III, had often quarrelled with her husband, complaining that he was insensitive. She resented especially the fact that he left the burden of most minor responsibilities and chores to her, while he was either too immersed in his work, or too tired to help, or too busy to remember. She acknowledged, however, that their relationship was basically warm and loyal, and she blamed herself for being oversensitive and irritable.
>
> As the treatment progressed, Mrs. Q. began to realize that she thwarted subtly but effectively her husband's occasional attempts to help or relieve the burden. We finally recognized her irresistible need to do everything for herself, and even more so, for others. She began to put a limit on her numerous family and public obligations.
>
> One day, as they were preparing to go abroad, Mrs. Q.'s husband commented: "You know, we are leaving in a few days and you haven't bought new suitcases yet." Mrs. Q. replied: "You are right. I am too busy, why don't you buy them yourself, otherwise, we will have to take the old ones." Mr. Q. was too dumbfounded to answer, but he duly went downtown and bought suitcases.
>
> Had that been a cognitive therapy we could have probably concluded that the topic was closed once the patient was able to contemplate and implement a different course of action. Since ours, however, was a dynamic psychotherapy, we wanted to know how such a bright, competent woman could have been so deficient in social skills, unable to share burdens rationally and take care of her own comfort. What transpired first was a need to control and dominate, and then an unconscious but strong need to feel exploited. This need went back to a real early childhood situation, but also served as a reaction-formation against the patient's own repressed greed. On a deeper level we were faced with an overwhelming oral rage of which the patient was deathly afraid. Now we realized why the patient was compelled to behave as she did: any other, more selfish attitude would bring about the threat of the repressed greed and rage breaking out.

As the patient begins to reexamine his personal style of behavior and its motives, he also begins to perceive the motivation of others more clearly, free of distortion or projection. His work- and love-relationships become assessed more realistically. The spouse is no longer the threatening mother nor the child the "bad", rejected part of oneself. The patient not only reassesses his present life and charts a new course for himself, he also takes a look at his past and re-writes his personal history.

All that is an imposing cognitive task and one of the reasons that analytic treatment takes so much time. Moreover, the cognitive process should not be seen as a mere tool of analysis; it has, as we have seen, an emotional significance of its own. The cognitive process mediated by the analyst is not only a component of transference. It is also a component of the therapeutic alliance, because the acquisition of insight is a realistic objective of psycho-analysis. Mediated learning, in childhood as well as in analysis, has a dual significance. On the one hand, it consolidates the symbiotic bond in the infant and fosters dependence in the patient. On the other hand, mediated learning in the infant promotes the development of skills which later facilitate separation-individuation and autonomy; in the patient the acquisition of insight facilitates the *resolution* of transference and promotes emotional growth.

The analyst, on his part, responds emotionally to the role of a mediating parent-teacher. It is essentially a gratifying role for the therapist as much as it is for the parent, and one may be easily enticed to engage in it more than is therapeutically useful. The enjoyment of mediated teaching is a narcissistic form of counter-transference, but a relatively benign one. A caring emotional relationship, such as parent-child or therapist-patient relationship, fosters the projection of narcissistic needs on the object of care. We enjoy helping the person we care for to develop his or her competence, because we re-live vicariously the joy of mastery we had experienced in our own childhood.

There is another, more destructive form of narcissistic counter-transference, which expresses a wish for power and fantasy of omniscience. It is essentially self-serving though it may be disguised under the intention to "give the patient the best he deserves". In the last analysis, it is an envious identification with the powerful and omiscient parent of the analyst's own childhood. Both forms of counter-transference reflect narcissistic needs but the routes taken by narcissism are entirely different and the effects on the treatment process are not identical.

Last but not least, the therapist is not only a teacher but also a learner. We learn a great deal from each analysis and often from a single session. Were it not so, few of us would be willing or able to endure the emotional demands of analytical work. For most of us, the gratification of learning is the main sustaining force of the vocational motivation. To put it in dry, technical terms: The positive affect generated by cognitive integration in the analyst's mind helps him to endure the frustrations of his task and to contain the negative affects projected on or deposited in him by the patient.

In conclusion, learning takes place from the beginning of life and throughout its duration. It involves an organization of perceptual, cognitive and emotional experiences and the integrative process itself generates a positive affect. Some learning is self-initiated, but much of it is "mediated" through the caregiver, the teacher, and, in patients, through the therapist. The gratification inherent in learning is derived from a narcissistic investment of ego functions. It is a significant component of the early object relationship, and later of a child's attachment to his teacher. In analysis, the gratification of learning is a component of the transference but also of the therapeutic alliance; it plays a significant role in sustaining the motivation for treatment, both in the patient and in the analyst.

CHAPTER TWELVE

A Comprehensive Approach to Child Development

The study of human development, like other scientific investigations, is becoming increasingly specialized. The vast amount of information generated by research defies the ability of a single human mind to absorb. Even more significantly, the refined methods for collecting and interpreting data cause the investigators to drift apart into ever more isolated fields of study, divided by barriers of terminology and conceptual frameworks.

Paradoxically, the spectacular advances of specialized developmental research reveal also its limitations. Specialized research achieves levels of validity and reliability unprecedented in the history of behavioral sciences, but the *meaning* of such findings can only emerge from a broad, comprehensive approach, cutting across the boundaries of individual disciplines. An experimental investigation may show *when* and *how* a certain function matures or a structure comes into being, but it will not explain *why*. A developmental sequence makes sense only when examined in the context of the functioning of the organism as a whole. For instance, the development of neural structures becomes meaningful when it correlates with behavioral development. It has been found that the cerebral cortex of a newborn guinea pig, which can move about, shows many more dendritic spines, than that of a newborn mouse, whose eyes are closed and which is comparatively much more helpless. However, at the age of two weeks, at a time when the mouse's eyes open, the density of dendritic spines in its cortex is similar to that of a newborn guinea pig (Schüz, 1978).

Correlations between processes occurring in diverse areas, such as neuroanatomy, behavior or intrapsychic development, have stimulated a search for more comprehensive perspectives of child development (Pine, 1985; Lichtenberg, 1983). One conspicuous correlation between various areas of development is *synchronization*. Many functions, some of them seemingly unrelated, show a synchronous pattern of development. In some cases the link is relatively simple: a certain function can only develop when another function reaches a certain level of maturation. For instance, a child begins to imitate speech after he acquires the ability to modulate his vocalizations, i.e., one skill constitutes the substrate for the other. In a similar manner, a degree of perceptual and cognitive maturity is needed for the child to establish self-boundaries and to separate from the symbiotic object, a process which will be described more fully later.

In other cases, the link is less direct and the maturation of a function is not à rigid prerequisite but it facilitates or stimulates progress in another area. For instance, locomotion (effective crawling or walking) facilitates separation-individuation (Mahler et al., 1975). A more organized discharge of aggressive drive facilitates negativistic or defiant behavior, which is also an important component of separation-individuation (McDevitt, 1983).

In still other cases, the relationship is indirect and not easily discernible, but nevertheless significant. Many developmental tasks depend on appropriate stimulation. In some cases, however, that stimulation is self-induced, i.e., the child manipulates the environment to produce the stimuli. For instance, Kermoian (1987) demonstrated that the development of a sense of direction depends on locomotion. Apparently, a child who explores his environment provides himself with visual, kinesthetic and proprioceptive stimuli which facilitate the mental representation of space. In children who could not walk, the sense of direction was delayed.

Synchronization of development stages may be due not to any link between them, but may have evolved as a result of adaptive pressures. It may be advantageous for an organism to complete a developmental task before reaching a turning point in another area of maturation. For instance, effective hand-mouth coordination appears at an age when the baby becomes ready for a mixed diet. In other words, a child becomes physically capable of feeding himself at a time when he is metabolically mature to make use of it. Another example of such adaptively useful synchronization is the juvenile appearance of animals. In many mammal and bird species the young individuals have a specific and conspicuous coloring of fur or feathers which protects them from attack by adult members of the species (Lorenz, 1968). That coloring disappears at a time when the animal leaves parental protection and becomes ready to fend for itself and compete for sexual partners.

In conclusion, a comprehensive model of human development should integrate at least five development lines:

(a) Somatic, especially neural structures and neurophysiological functions;
(b) Sensory processes and motor behaviors;
(c) Cognitive processes;
(d) Emotional processes and intrapsychic structures;
(e) Interpersonal relationships and social behavior.

Such a model ought to express the complex reciprocal relationships between the various developmental lines at each stage. Moreover, it ought to present all developmental sequences and their synchronization in an ethological perspective, i.e., explicate their adaptive and survival values.

Today such an integrated model of human development is an unreachable goal, even though more and more clinicians and experimental investigators attempt to formulate their ideas in a form that crosses inter-disciplinary boundaries. The study of developmental deviations is a particularly fruitful area on which to base a preliminary outline of a comprehensive developmental model. As often happens, the disruption of a process provides more insight into its internal organization than mere observation of its smooth, normal course. Therefore, our discussion of developmental synchronization will rely to a considerable extent on the observations of developmental deviations. Some examples of synchronization and its failure have been mentioned in Chapter Six; here we examine the issue in a more systematic manner.

We view development as a continuous process of progressive differentiation and organization (Werner, 1961; Werner and Kaplan, 1963). Differentiation consists of acquisition of new functions or the transformation of a simple function into a more complex one, i.e., substitution of lower level by higher level functions. For instance, a small child can learn to recite from memory a sequence of numbers from one to ten. For an older child these numbers signify a quantity: five children, seven applies. For a still older child numbers are components of arithmetical operations. In such a way the concept becomes more complex as a result of differentiation.

Organization means integration of the new function into a harmoniously operating whole. The conceptual framework of differentiation and integration is related to, but not synonymous with Piaget's concepts of assimilation and accomodation (Piaget, 1952).

The living organism, especially the immature one, becomes progressively differentiated. Environmental pressures impinge on the growing organism and cause it to change, but they are not the sole determinants of differentiation. A living organism is a *self-organizing* system (Stechler, 1982). It is endowed with an irresistible pull to absorb and process information in order to enhance its own complexity and organization. This pre-programmed need can be compared to the need of a developing organism to absorb matter and energy in order to enhance its physical size and complexity.

Most psychoanalysts and clinicians describe the infant as an organism which is not yet integrated. This, in our view, is misleading. If integration means inner harmony and adaptability to the environment, then a healthy newborn infant is exquisitely integrated: well balanced, equipped to evoke in a compelling manner the appropriate ministrations from his caregivers, and capable of making use of those ministrations effectively. A newborn infant is, however, relatively undifferentiated, i.e., his functional repertoire is modest and simple, and it cannot restore its integration once that has been disrupted, without external help. The newborn's functional repertoire is focussed on two main goals: survival and development.

We propose to describe the stages of child development in terms of *developmental objectives*. By "objective" we mean the acquisition of a higher level of organization in the sphere of cognition, behavior or regulatory functions, i.e., intrapsychic structures. We de-emphasize, in this discussion, specific chronological norms. We do so not because we underestimate their clinical and scientific importance, but because we are concerned here primarily with the processes and the relationships, and not with chronological tables. We also recognize the wide individual differences in consolidating developmental objectives and the considerable overlapping of stages. It often happens that the groundwork for a certain objective is being laid long before the previous objective becomes fully consolidated.

A. The oral-symbiotic stage

The *intra-psychic* objective of this stage, which covers roughly the first year of life, is the formation of symbiosis, that is, a strongly preferential, sometimes exclusive, bond to a caregiver. This stage is characterized by two major *cognitive* objectives, namely, recognition of the familiar and contingent, or instrumental, learning.

Recognition of the familiar is an obligatory precondition for the formation of a symbiotic bond. We have already discussed in the previous chapter the reciprocal relationship between recognition and affect. In brief, the positive affect that accompanies need-relieving ministrations helps the child to recognize the caregiver, while the recognition of the familiar *in itself* generates a positive affect which contributes to the attachment to the familiar caregiver (Chapter Eleven).

Recognition of a familiar percept, called by some investigators "declarative" memory, is a function which matures during the first months of life and is located primarily in the limbic system (Bachevalier and Mishkin, 1984). That, in itself, is an interesting finding. The limbic system is the primary center of affect-regulation and such a close anatomic proximity of the two functions, i.e., affect regulation and recognition of the familiar, parallels Papoušek's studies on recognition and affect.

Lesions of the limbic system cause impairment of recognition memory in monkeys. In infant monkeys they cause, in addition, a syndrome resembling early infantile autism. That finding also demonstrates the close relationship between recognition and object-relationship (Merjanian et al., 1986).

In conclusion, the attainment of the main developmental objective of the first year, i.e., the symbiotic bond, requires, besides empathic and affectionate caregiving, the synchronous maturation of several functions: perceptual ability, "declarative" memory and an adequate affective response on the part of the infant. An infant who fails to respond to familiar percepts with pleasure may encounter difficulties in establishing a symbiotic bond.

The next two steps in cognitive development are contingent learning, i.e., recognizing the lawful association between two percepts, and operant, or instrumental conditioning, i.e., learning that a behavior initiated by the infant produces a specific result. Both these processes are intrinsically pleasurable (see Chapter Eleven). Infants disregard blithely Pavlov's injunction never to refer to emotional states when studying conditioned responses. For infants conditioning games are sheer joy. It is not surprising, therefore, that *pleasure in the task performed* is a better predictor of intellectual functioning at the age of three than any other measure of infant behavior (Birns and Golden, 1972).

We can offer a speculative hypothesis about the mechanism by which affect facilitates cognitive development. Greenough, et al. (1987) have suggested an original neurophysiological model of learning. They present evidence to show that learning occurs by stabilization of active synapses and by erasure of inactive redundant ones. Some information-processing systems are "experience-expectant", i.e., preprogrammed to receive "expectable" stimuli from what the authors call an average expectable environment for that particular species. "Experience-expectant" systems mature according to a predetermined chronological sequence, which may well constitute the neuroanatomic basis for critical periods of mental development.

Learning also occurs as a result of individual, unexpected or even idiosyncratic experiences. Such "experience-dependent" learning occurs, according to Greenough, because there is always a redundance of synapses. Moreover, synaptic proliferation continues, albeit at a diminishing rate, throughout life. Environmental stimulation, according to Greenough, may increase the rate of proliferation, possibly by activating the alerting system. We assume that affect, or more accurately the neurophysiological processes, which underlie affect, might serve to stabilize synapses and to stimulate their proliferation.

That hypothesis could account for the role of affect in cognition, because positive affect would stabilize *successful* cognitive operations, while absence of positive affect, or negative affect, could lead to the erasure of synaptic connections that were responsible for *unsuccessful* operations.

According to that hypothesis, when infants and caregivers engage in learning games, such as reciprocal smiling, exchanging sounds, or imitating movements, they activate a process (pleasurable affect) that stabilizes the neural circuits involved in those operations. In such a manner the learning games help to consolidate the attachment to the caregiver and at the same time enhance the differentiation of perceptual, motor and cognitive functions.

In conclusion, the main objective of the first stage of emotional development, i.e., the formation of the symbiotic bond, is linked to the maturation of the limbic system of recognition memory. It is also linked to the affective processes that accompany early cognition. It is possible that affects determine the stabilization and erasure of synapses and thus shape early learning processes.

B. Individuation: The emergence of self

The next major developmental objective is individuation, i.e., the emergence and consolidation of self-representation. It is reasonable to assume that the early nucleus of self-representation is the body-self, i.e., the gradually emerging mental image of the infant's own body (Freud, 1923). The body-image, it is generally assumed, emerges from the repeated perception of simultaneous stimuli: tactile, proprioceptive, visual and kinesthetic. These convergent stimuli recur in lawful patterns, e.g., if I move my arm in a certain manner, my hand will appear invariably before my eyes. Touching my own body evokes two tactile stimuli, while touching anything else evokes only one.

The convergence of proprioceptive and tactile stimuli begins probably during intra-uterine existence. We are inclined to believe that a major milestone toward the construction of body image occurs with the emergence of "midline behavior", i.e., when the infant learns to move his hands intentionally into and out of his visual field, and to make them touch under visual control.

In conclusion, the earliest nucleus of self-representation, i.e., the body-image, consists of engrams of motor and perceptual processes, and depends on their maturation.

The next step toward self-representation is cognitive. Stechler (1982) observed that infants become capable of organizing a goal-directed plan of action during the latter part of the first of life. Such a plan of action may be delayed or modified during its implementation if the circumstances demand it. The observer, nevertheless, gets a clear impression that no matter what bypasses are needed, the child knows very well what he wants and he pursues the goal in a stepwise fashion. Stechler suggested that the mental representations of a wish and of a goal-directed, organized plan of action constitute the very beginning of self-awareness (Stechler, 1982), the beginning of meta-cognition. It is not merely "I want", but "I know that I want".

The next step on the road to individuality is separation, i.e., "I want, but Mother does not". That constellation also begins in some infants toward the end of the first year, but reaches its peak during the second year of life with the advent of effective locomotion. The older infant or the toddler makes an astounding discovery: it is no longer a question of mother being or not being in his visual field; now *he* can disappear from mother's visual field as well! That momentous discovery endows the toddler with a new sense of power. He has already learned to manipulate objects and overcome obstacles; now he can exert some power over his omnipotent parent as well! Maturation of gross motility allows also the toddler to express aggression in a more organized way.

At this point we need to make a digression and present an outine of the development of aggressive discharge. We divide the development of aggression not according to the somatic systems involved (as is the case of psychosexual development), but according to the level of organization. We distinguish the following stages:

(1) Global undifferentiated response, manifested by aimless, diffuse movements, crying, changes in skin color, heart rate and other visceral changes. It is a poorly differentiated

state and some of its components can be seen in other, even pleasurable, excitatory states.

(2) Behavioral response: During the latter part of the first year babies acquire the ability to respond to frustration by intentional movements, such as pushing or throwing. They learn to defend their possessions from their peers' acquisitive intentions and may discourage an intruder by a well-timed preemptive pull of his or her hair.

The ability to express aggression effectively by intentional movements develops quickly during the second year of life. The child can hit, bite and throw objects either away or at someone.

(3) Verbal discharge, i.e., expressing an angry affect or aggressive wish in words. The lower level of verbal discharge is shouting *at* someone, or "throwing" insults; in other words, using speech as a means of attack. The higher level is represented by verbal expressions of angry affect, e.g., "I resent what you have done".

(4) Cognitive working through: That is a unique form of dealing with aggressive impulses, since no external release of drive is involved. Those favorable instances when insight into transference or counter-transference resolves the patient's or, respectively, the therapist's anger, are examples of cognitive working-through. We do not know the precise mechanism of this process, but it is an additional example of the basic connection between cognitive and affective processes.

The transition from one stage of aggressive discharge to another depends on maturation, but it is facilitated by environmental influences, especially "mediating" influence of the caregivers. The caregiver comforts and restrains, "holds" the infant and facilitates modulation and differentiation of the diffuse neonatal responses. Later, parents guide and moderate the toddler's behavioral responses and help the child to acquire the skills of verbal expression. In other words, the caregivers facilitate the differentiation of aggressive discharge and determine, to a considerable extent, its final form.

Let us return now to the process of individuation. McDevitt (1983) described the role of behavioral aggression during the phase of separation-individuation. Early aggressive responses, according to him, do not manifest an intent to hurt but they promote distancing from the mother and self-object differentiation.

Aggressive responses in the toddler, especially oppositional behavior, which is so characteristic at that stage, are the toddler's main tools for delineating his "territory" and asserting his autonomy. A toddler has few skills to prove himself: he can neither express himself in words nor sing, nor to draw a picture as pretty as that of Big Sister, nor read a newspaper like Father. He can, however, assert his individuality by being stubborn and getting into confrontations. The maturation of language and other skills cause the aggressive and oppositional behaviors to abate.

The outcome of the power struggles of the stage of individuation depends as much on maternal responsiveness as on the child's developmental individuality. Impulsive, drive-dominated children make it difficult for the mother to respond with optimum restraint. Children with slow motor development are more inclined to remain passive and dependent, and so are the children whose mothers are excessively harsh. In other words, innate or environmental factors may lead to similar results.

An unresolved "battle of wills" of the separation-individuation stage leads to an internalization of the conflict of wills, manifested by ambivalence and struggle of conflicting tendencies, that is compulsive personality traits.

In conclusion, the stage of individuation is ushered by perceptual and motor maturation. Its normal course is facilitated by the onset of locomotion and by organization of aggressive discharge in the form of behavioral aggressive response.

C. The Oedipal stage

The main developmental objectives of the Oedipal stage are:

(a) A differential emotional relationship with each of the important people in the child's nuclear family: parents primarily, but also siblings or auxiliary caregivers.

(b) Ambivalence, that is the ability to contain opposite affective tendencies, love and hate, directed at the same object. This is different from the fleeting affective states of the younger child, insofar as now both affects *persist*, even though one may dominate at any given moment.

(c) The ability to engage the parent, especially the parent of the opposite sex, in a *competitive* rather than *negativistic* confrontation.

(d) Identification with parental figures, including gender identity and super-ego consolidation (Chapter Six).

The development of the psychic apparatus during the Oedipal stage is more autonomous than it was in the preceding stages, less closely linked to motor and cognitive maturation and more under the influence of interpersonal and cultural factors. There is a considerable individual variability in the content and duration of the Oedipal stage, and its limits, especially its termination, are less clearly defined. As a result, the synchronization of Oedipal objectives with other developmental milestones is much less conspicuous than it was in the pre-Oedipal stages. Nevertheless, some connections between Oedipal objectives on the one hand, and cognitive and motor maturation on the other, can be discerned.

The first connection between cognitive development and Oedipal objectives has to do with categories. The development of differential relationships and of gender identity requires categorical thinking. The little child has to recognize qualities inherent in an implicit category in order to organize his world of relationships, even though he is not yet capable of making a formal definition of that category. "Me and Daddy are boys, Anna and Mommy are girls. Daddy and Mommy are grown-ups, me and Anna are kids. Kids don't drive cars, boys don't have babies." Children of preschool age are not generally considered capable of constructing categories, except those based on simple, concrete qualities, such as edibility or appearance. Preschool children are also not considered capable of inductive reasoning. That is not quite correct. Gelman and her associates have conducted a series of studies on categorical and inferential reasoning in children. In one such study (Gelman & Markman, 1987) they found that children aged three and four can make correct inferences when dealing with "natural kinds" categories. "Natural kinds" are objects found in nature, such as animals. For instance, a child is shown a picture of a little brown snake and told that it lays eggs. Then it is shown pictures of other animals and asked if they can lay eggs, too. Most children infer correctly that a cobra lays eggs, while a brown worm, similar in appearance and color to the little snake, does not.

Adults, children, male and female, are all "natural kinds"; categories that include more than mere perceptual features. An older child might be bigger than a small adult, and yet children consider him "a kid"; therefore, it becomes apparent that an Oedipal child needs to have reached the conceptual competence to categorize "natural kinds" and use inductive reasoning in order to organize his world of relationships.

Another important contribution to the Oedipal stage is provided by motor and language development. An Oedipal child needs to confront his parents in a *competitive* manner. To do so he needs a considerable measure of self-confidence and also the ability to imitate at least some adult behaviors. Both these requirements are facilitated by the rapid spurt in language and motor development which takes place in the third and fourth years of life. A three or four year old child can express his wishes verbally, can recount events, sing, sometimes better than his parent, and engage in a sensible conversation. He has all the basic *motor* skills of the adult and needs only to refine them. He does not have the strength nor judgment needed to hunt a buffalo or drive an automobile, but he can climb a suitably constructed ladder with an agility equal to or surpassing that of the average middle-aged adult. Therefore, a competitive confrontation with the parent can be entertained, even though it is but seldom crowned with success.

In conclusion, cognitive maturation, namely, the ability to infer from a "natural kind" category, facilitates the differential object relationship that characterizes the Oedipal stage. Verbal and motor development facilitate the transition from oppositional to competitive confrontation.

D. Latency

Latency involves a decrease in the intensity of emotional ties with the early objects and turning away toward peer relationships, and social and cognitive pursuits. Shapiro et al. (1976) concluded that there is no evidence of a decrease in the absolute strength of drives; the decrease is *relative* since cognitive and social skills expand rapidly and social interests predominate. In other words, maturation does determine the onset of latency, but in a way different from what had been assumed.

In summary, the development of what is sometimes called "ego-apparatuses", namely, perception, motility and cognition, is inextricably enmeshed with emotional development, maturation of drives, and the formation of psychic structures. "Ego apparatuses" do not develop in a rigid, predetermined order: the growing organism explores the world actively in order to supply itself with stimuli which assure the optimal development of "ego apparatuses", and affects are the movers and facilitators of this process. The relationship between emotional development and "ego apparatuses" is reciprocal. Affects stimulate and shape the development of "ego apparatuses", while the synchronized maturation of perception, motility and cognition assures the progressive acquisition of intrapsychic developmental objectives.

CHAPTER THIRTEEN

Conclusions

Major advances in science occur for one of the following reasons:

(a) A new instrument or a new method for collecting data leads to restructuring of the theory; or
(b) Advances in other sciences provide fresh data and new concepts that enrich the existing theories, without diminishing their validity.

The revolution in biology brought about by the microscope or the blossoming of learning theory as a result of conditioning experiments are examples of the first kind of advance. The impact of the biological theory of evolution on social sciences is an example of the second kind of advance, i.e., of input from one science enriching another one.

Psychoanalysis has always been open to input from a wide range of sciences and humanities. Freud's models of the mind were inspired by the neurological theory of Hughlings Jackson, while his insight into child sexuality was inspired by Sophocles. In order to maintain its vitality, psychoanalysis needs to maintain its openness to other sciences, because psychoanalysis depends almost exclusively on one method for collecting data, i.e., on the psychoanalytic treatment process. Therefore it is quite natural that many analysts maintain a vivid interest in other behavioral sciences and in humanities.

In spite of all that has been said, the impact of the vast amount of developmental research of the last four decades on psychoanalytic theory is modest and its impact on clinical practice even less. The reason seems to be twofold: The first is a vague preconception that biologically-determined phenomena are immutable and therefore untreatable by psychological means. We hope to have demonstrated here that the opposite is true, i.e., that the interaction between innate and environmental forces provides ample opportunities for successful interventions. The other difficulty lies in the language gap between psychoanalysis and other behavioral sciences. Some concepts seem related, e.g., "operant conditioning" may lead to a situation called "fixation". The concepts, however, are defined in such totally alien ways that one can never be certain to what extent they describe the same phenomenon.

Moreover, psychoanalysis itself is not a monolithic body of theories and some analysts have coined their own terms to describe their personal hypotheses. The difficulties of a theoretical integration between psychoanalysis and developmental theory can be seen in Lichtenberg's (1983) scholarly study. In our experience it is more feasible and probably more useful to integrate psychoanalytic and neuropsychological approaches in the context of a specific clinical problem or an individual case, before attempting integration on a theoretical level.

What is to be gained from including neuropsychological and developmental considerations into clinical psychoanalytic work? In our opinion, the benefits are the following:

(a) The better one understands the patient, and that includes, for instance, his or her cognitive difficulties, the stronger is the therapeutic alliance;

(b) Neuropsychological impairments and their effects account for a significant proportion of therapeutic failures. Whenever treatment seems to have reached an impasse and a problem does not yield to interpretations, the possibility of an unrecognized developmental issue needs to be considered.

(c) The therapist's attempts to modify a behavioral trait without recognizing its innate nature, perpetuate the parent's futile efforts to eradicate it. The parents tried to do so by persuasion or pressure; the therapist offers interpretations, but the patient's subjective experience is identical. He feels misunderstood and helpless. It is only after we recognize the innate nature of the trait, that we can ask the patient to decide whether to modify it or accept it as ego-syntonic.

(d) Insight into a patient's developmental individuality adds a significant dimension to psychoanalytic reconstruction.

Freud (1937b) compared reconstruction in psychoanalysis to archeological excavation, the assumption being that the analyst's efforts, however fallible and subject to bias, are aimed at events that actually occurred. This striving for objectivity has been challenged recently. For instance, Schwaber (1986) gave examples of distortions inherent in an analyst's reconstructive work and emphasized the importance of the patient's subjective experience. We do not agree with such a relativistic attitude to reconstruction.

It is certainly true that reconstruction is created by the analyst as much as a historical study is a creation of the historian's mind. This, however, does not justify dismissing the historian's quest for the elusive truth as "naive realism". A patient's recollections combine facts and fantasy, but the analyst can and should help in an approximative reassessment of the past. He can do so by contributing his knowledge of developmental processes and of developmental aberrations, and their effects on the child and his environment. The deep relief experienced by the patient whose hurt, fears and bewilderment begin to make sense, is a most convincing vindication of the quest for objectivity.

Finally, we would like to make a general comment on the therapeutic approach to the patient with developental deviations. Small (1980) published a scholarly and lucid exposition of the problems and promises of neuropsychological aspects of diagnosis and treatment. Our approach differs in some important ways from his contribution, perhaps because most of our patients manifested only subtle and circumscribed impairments of cognitive or integrative functions which do not merit the diagnosis of a "sub-clinical brain lesion" as most of his cases did. Therefore, our patients' problem was not to so much the neuropsychological deficit *in itself* as it was the impact of the deviation on the emotional development and object relationships. Our treatment strategy is not a *choice* between dynamic interpretation and coping with the neuropsychological problem, but a *combination* of both. Our approach is primarily developmental. We ask not only *what* went wrong and *why*, but also *when*. In other words, what was the life situation and what were the developmental tasks that had been affected by the impairment of an ego function.

The developmental approach in psychotherapy and psychoanalysis will be facilitated by sharing the knowledge between developmental investigators and psychoanalysts, a process that has already begun. It will also be facilitated when more psychoanalytic institutes and training facilities for psychotherapy include child observations and child studies in their program. As therapists we have come to believe that an extensive working experience with young children and their parents facilitates a more vivid, more emotionally intense, empathic identification with the patient's childhood reminiscences. It also facilitates insight into the role of the parent. It is certainly true that analysis opens the gate to childhood, but it is equally true that understanding children's world opens the gate to psychoanalysis.

References

Aleksandrowicz, M.K. The biological strangers: An attempted suicide of a seven-and-a-half year old girl. Bull. Menn. Clin., 1975a, 39/2, 163–176.

Aleksandrowicz, M.K. The Little Prince: Psychotherapy of a boy with borderline personality structure. Int. J. Psychoan. Psychother., 1975b, 4/16, 410–425.

Aleksandrowicz, M.K. & Aleksandrowicz, D.R. Obstetrical pain-relieving drugs as predictors of infant behavior variability. Child Devel., 1974, 45/4, 935–946.

Aleksandrowicz, M.K. & Aleksandrowicz, D.R. Case history of a happy child. Child Psychiat. & Human Dev., 1975a, 5/3, 174–181.

Aleksandrowicz, M.K. & Aleksandrowicz, D.R. The molding of personality: A newborn's innate characteristics in interaction with parents' personalities. Child Psychiat. & Hum. Dev., 1975b, 5/4, 231–241.

Aleksandrowicz, M.K. & Aleksandrowicz, D.R. Precursors of ego in neonates: Factor analysis of Brazelton Scale data. J. Amer. Acad. Child Psychiat., 1976, 15/2, 257–268.

Aleksandrowicz, M.K. & Aleksandrowicz, D.R. The Palm Hill project: A field experiment in early intervention in a disadvantaged Israeli community. Bull. Menn. Clin., 1987, 15/2, 133–143.

Aleksandrowicz, D.R., Davis, M. and Aleksandrowicz, M.K. Self-esteem in learning-disabled children. VI. Natl. Mtg. Isr. Psychiat. Assn., Ramat Gan, May 10–12, 1988.

Andrulonis, P.A., Glueck, B.C., Stroebel, C.F. & Vogel, N.G. Borderline personality subcategories. J. Nerv. Ment. Dis., 1982, 170/11, 670–679.

Ausubel, D. and Sullivan, E. Theories and problems of child development. 2nd ed., New York: Grune and Stratton, 1970.

Bachevalier, J. & Mishkin, M. An early and a late developing system for learning and retention in infant monkeys. Beh. Neurosci., 1984, 98/5, 770–778.

Bayley, N. Bayley Scales of Infant Development. New York: Psychol. Corp., 1969.

Bergman, P. & Escalona, S.K. Unusual sensitivities in very young children. Psychoanal. Study Child, 1949, 3–4, 333–352.

Birns, B. & Golden, M. Prediction of intellectual performance at three years from infant tests and personality measures. Merril-Palmer Quart., 1972, 18, 53–58.

Blum, H.P. The value of reconstruction in adult psychoanalysis. Int. J. Psychoanal., 1980, 61, 39–52.

116 REFERENCES

Brackbill, Y. Obstetrical medication and infant behavior. In: Handbook of Infant Development, ed. J.D. Osofsky. New York: Wiley and Sons, 1979, pp. 76–125.

Brazelton, T.B. Neonatal Behavioral Assessment Scale. Philadelphia: Lippincott, 1973.

Bridges, K. Emotional development in early infancy. Child Dev. 1932, 3, 324–341.

Coopersmith, S. The Antecedents of Self-Esteem. San Francisco: W.H. Freeman, 1967.

Diagnostic and Statistical Manual of Mental Disorders, 3rd ed., revised. Washington, D.C.: Amer. Psychiat. Assn., 1987.

Elliott, F.A. Neurological findings in adult minimal brain dysfunction and the dyscontrol syndrome. J. Nerv. Ment. Dis., 1982, 170/11, 680–687.

Erikson, E.H. Childhood and Society. New York: Norton, 1950.

Escalona, S.K. The Roots of Individuality: Normal Patterns of Development in Infancy. Chicago: Aldine, 1968.

Escalona, S.K. & Heider, G.M. Prediction and Outcome. New York: Basic Books, 1959.

Feuerstein, R. The Dynamic Assessment of Retarded Performers: The Learning Potential, Assessment Device, Theory, Instruments and Techniques. Baltimore; University Park Press, 1979.

Freud, S. (1918) From the History of an Infantile Neurosis. Standard Edition (SE), 17, 3–123, London: Hogarth, 1955.

Freud, S. (1920) Beyond the pleasure principle. SE, 18, 14–16, London: Hogarth, 1955.

Freud, S. (1923) The Ego and the Id. SE, 19, 1–59, London: Hogarth, 1961.

Freud, S. (1937a) Analysis terminable and interminable. SE, 23 209–253, London: Hogarth, 1964.

Freud, S. (1937b) Constructions in analysis. SE, 23, 255–269, London: Hogarth, 1964.

Fries, M.E. & Woolf, P.J. Some hypotheses on the role of the congenital activity type in personality development. Psa. Study Child, 1953, 8, 48–62.

Gelman, S.A. & Markman, E.M. Young children's inductions from natural kinds: The role of categroies and appearances. Child Dev., 1987, 58/6, 1532–1541.

Gillberg, C., Rasmussen, P., Carlstrom, G., Svenson, B. & Waldenstrom, E. Perceptual, motor and attentional deficits in six-year-old children: Epidemiological aspects. J. Child Psychol. & Psychiat., 1982, 23/2, 131–144.

Greenough, W.T., Black, J.E. & Wallace, C.S. Experience and brain development. Child Dev., 1987, 58, 539–559.

Hunt, J. McV. Intrinsic motivation and its role in development. In: Levine, D. (ed.), Nebraska Symposium on Motivation, vol. 13. Lincoln, NE: University of Nebraska, 1965, pp. 189–282.

Kanner, L. Childhood Psychosis: Initial Studies and New Insights. Washington: Winston, 1973.

Karmiloff-Smith, A. From meta-processes to conscious access: Evidence from children's metalinguistic and repair data. Cognition, 1986, 23, 95–147.

Kermoian, R. Locomotor experience and spatial search. Biennial Mtg. Developmental Psychobiology Research Group. Estes Park, CO, 1986.

Kernberg, O.F. The treatment of patients with borderline personality organization. Int. J. Psychoanal., 1968, 49, 600–619.

Kernberg, O.F. Borderline Conditions and Pathological Narcissism. New York: Aronson, 1975.

Kernberg, O.F. Internal World and External Reality. New York: Aronson, 1980.

Kernberg, O.F. Object-relations Theory and Clinical Psychoanalysis. New York: Aronson, 1984.

Kernberg, P. Update of borderline disorders in children. Occup. Ther. in Mental Health, 1983, 3, 83–91.

Kestenberg, J. & Buelte, A. Prevention, infant therapy and the treatment of adults: (I) Toward understanding mutuality. Int. J. Psychoanal. Psychother., 1977, 6, 339–396.

Kestenberg, J.S., Marcus, H., Robbins, E., Berlowe, J. & Buelte, A. Development of the young child as expressed through bodily movement, I. J. Amer. Psychoanal. Assn., 1971, 19/4, 746–764.

Koester, L.S., Papoušek, H. & Papoušek, M. Psychobiological models of infant development: Influences on the concept of intuitive parenting. In: H. Rank and H. Ch. Steinhausen (eds.), Psychobiology and Early Development. North-Holland: Elsevier, 1987.

Kohlberg, L. Stage and sequence: The cognitive-developmental approach to socialization. In: D. Goslin (ed.), Handbook of Socialization Theory. Chicago: rand McNally, 1969.

Kohut, H. The Analysis of the Self. New York: Int. Univ. Press, 1971.

Korner, A.F. Some hypotheses regarding the significance of individual differences at birth for later development. Psa. Study Child, 1964, 19, 58–72.

Korner, A.F. Individual differences at birth: Implications for early experience and later development. Amer. J. Orthopsychiat., 1971, 41/4, 608–619.

Korner, A.F. & Grobstein, R. Individual differences at birth: Implications for mother-infant relations and later development. J. Amer. Acad. Child Psychiat., 1967, 6, 676–690.

Lamb, M.E. (ed.) The Role of the Father in Child Development. New York: Wiley, 1981.

Lichtenberg, J.D. Psychoanalysis and Infant Research. Hillsdale, NJ: The Analytic Press (Lawrence Erlbaum Ass.), 1983.

Lishman, W.A. Organic Psychiatry: The Psychological Consequences of Cerebral Disorder, 2nd ed. Oxford: Blackwell, 1987.

Liss, E. Motivations in learning. Psychoanal. Study Child, 1955, 10, 100–116.

Lorenz, K. On Aggression. London: Methuen, 1968.

Luria, A.R. Restoration of Function after Brain Injury. New York: Macmillan, 1963.

Mahler, M. & Goslinger, R. On symbiotic child psychosis: Genetic, dynamic and restitutive aspects. Psa. Study Child, 1955, 10, 195–212.

Mahler, M.S. & McDevitt, J.B. Thoughts on the emergence of the sense of self, with particular emphasis on the body self. J. Amer. Psychoanal., 1982, 30/4, 827–848.

Mahler, M., Pine, F. & Bergman, A. The Psychological Birth of the Human Infant. New York: Basic Books, 1975.

McDevitt, J.B. The emergence of hostile aggression and its defensive and adaptive modifications during the separation-individuation process. J. Amer. Psychoanal. Assn., 1983, 31 (suppl.), 273–300.

Mendelson, W., Johnson, N. & Stewart, M. Hyperactive children as teenagers: A follow-up study. J. Nerv. Ment. Dis., 1971, 153, 273–279.

Merjanian, P.M., Bachevalier, J., Crawford, H. & Mishkin, M. Socio-emotional disturtances in the developing rhesus monkey following neonatal limbic lesions. Soc. Neurosci. Abstract, 1986.

Murray, M.E. Minimal brain dysfunction and borderline personality adjustment. Amer. J. Psychother., 1979, 33/3, 391–403.

Osofsky, J.D. Handbook of Infant Development, 2nd ed. New York: Wiley-Interscience, 1987.

Palombo, J. Perceptual deficits and self-esteem in adolescence. Clin. Soc. Work J., 1979, 7, 34–61.

Palombo, J. Critical review of the concept of the borderline child. Clin. Soc. Work J., 1982, 10, 246–263.

Papoušek, H. & Papoušek, M. Biological basis of social interactions: Implications of research for an understanding of behavioral deviance. J. Child Psychol. & Psychiat., 1983, 24/1, 117–129.

Piaget, J. The Origins of Intelligence in Children. New York: Int. Univ. Press, 1952.

Pine, F. Developmental Theory and Clinical Process. New Haven: Yale Univ. Press, 1985.

Rubin, E.Z., Braun, J.S., Beck, G.R. & Llorens, L.A. Cognitive Perceptual Motor Dysfunction. Detroit, MI: Wayne State Univ., 1972.

Rutter, M. Separation, loss and family relationships. In: M. Rutter & L. Hersov (eds.), Child Psychiatry: Modern Approach. Oxford: Blackwell, 1977, pp. 47–73.

Schaeffer, H. & Emerson, P. Patterns of response to physical contact in early human development. J. Child Psychol. & Psychiat., 1964, 5, 1–13.

Schüz, A. Some facts and hypotheses concerning dendritic spines and learning. In: M.A.B. Brazier & H. Petsche (eds.), Architectionics of the Cerebral Cortex. New York: Raven Press, 1978, pp. 129–135.

Schwaber, E.A. Reconstruction and perceptual experience: Further thoughts on psychoanalytic listening. J. Amer. Psychoanal. Assn., 1986, 34/4, 911–932.

Shapiro, T. & Perry, R. Latency revisited: The age 7 plus or minus 1. Psychoanal. Study Child, 1976, 31, 79–105.

Small, L. Neuropsychodiagnosis in Psychotherapy. New York: Brunner-Mazel, 1973.

Sroufe, A. Socio-emotional development. In: J. Osofsky (ed.), Handbook of Infant Development. New York: Wiley, 1979, pp. 462–516.

Stechler, G. The dawn of awareness. Psychoanal. Inquiry, 1982, 1/4, 503–531.

St. Exupery, A. de, The Little Prince. New York: Harcourt, Brace & Co., 1943.

Thomas, A. & Chess. S. Temperament and Development. New York: Brunner-Mazel, 1977.

Thomas, A., Chess, S. & Birch. H.G. Temperament and Behavior Disorders in Children. New York: New York Univ. Press, 1968.

Weil, A.P. Maturational variations and genetic-dynamic issues. J. Amer. Psychoanal. Assn., 1978, 26/3, 461–491.

Weil, A.P. Anxiety in childhood: Developmental and psychopathological considerations. In: E. Anthony & D.C. Gilpin (eds.), Three Further Clinical Faces of Childhood. New York: Spectrum, 1981, pp. 135–149.

Wender, P.H. Minimal Brain Dysfunction in Children. New York: Wiley-Interscience, 1971.

Weiss, G., Hechtman, L. & Perlman, T. Hyperactives as young adults. Amer. J. Orthopsychiat., 1978, 48, 438–445.

Werner, H. Comparative Psychology of Mental Development. New York: Science Ed., 1961.

Werner, H. & Kaplan, B. Symbol Formation: An Organismic-developmental Approach to Language and Expression of Thought. New York: Wiley, 1963.

White, R.W. Motivation reconsidered: The concept of competence. Psychol. Rev., 1959, 66, 297–333.

Winnicott, D.W. Mirror-role of mother and family in child development. In: P. Lomas (ed.), The Predicament of the Family: A Psychoanalytical symposium. London: Hogarth, 1967.

Wolff, P.H. Observations on newborn infants. Psychosom. Med., 1959, 21, 110–118.

Wolff, P.H. The Causes, Control and Organization of Behavior in the Newborn. Psychol. Issues Monogr. 7. New York: Int. Univ. Press, 1966.

Index

DATE DUE